LT CO
PURCHASE

LT COLONEL PUROHIT
THE MAN BETRAYED?

SMITA MISHRA

Vitasta

Published by
Renu Kaul Verma
Vitasta Publishing Pvt Ltd
2/15, Ansari Road, Daryaganj
New Delhi - 110 002
info@vitastapublishing.com

ISBN: 978-93-90961-39-9
© Smita Mishra
First Edition 2023
MRP ₹ 399

Edited by Kanagam King
Typeset & Cover Design by Somesh Kumar Mishra
Printed by Vikas Computer and Printers, New Delhi

To all the unnamed and unknown intelligence personnel who put their lives on the line every day defending our country

Contents

Preface   *ix*

First Day, First Meet   1

It's Hindu Terror!   17

Abhinav Bharat   63

One Arrest, Many Questions   82

Torture Files   111

The Better Half   124

The Salve Perspective   146

Why Purohit?   158

The NIA Act Vs The Communal Violence Bill   167

Photo Gallery   *182*

Preface

My first exposure to so-called Hindu terror was like many other contemporary news reporters who were tasked to write on the cases and the political slugfest following them as a matter of daily news. At the outset, my interest in the subject was also limited to that. After all, it certainly was big news. The world of news reporting, which may appear very 'happening' to outsiders, has its own monotony. With most stories hovering around the 'he said, she said' limits, any twist in the tale is welcome.

However, what started as just another interesting issue to watch out for, soon became quite baffling. It started one fine morning with breaking news on the Malegaon blasts and then incident after incident, in quick succession, started getting labelled as Hindu terror. It was all happening so fast it became difficult to catch up. What was even more baffling was that incidents where Jihadi organisations had been found openly involved and investigations were at an advanced state were also billed as Hindu Terror after curious U-turns.

It was a hectic but puzzling time for reporters. But even as new 'revelations' kept spilling out from various sources (some political, some agencies), there was a lot that didn't add up. Islamic terror or Jihad is a reality and the whole world has been dealing with the challenge for quite a long time. But Hindu terror seemed to have suddenly sprung up overnight. In a matter of days, it seemed as if an organisation or group of people had penetrated to all four corners of the country and carried out fatal blasts. The whole thing appeared fantastic. And yet there was news of fresh evidence coming out every day.

Like many others, my mind too was full of questions. When my friend Renu said it was a waste to just talk about it and suggested that I must work further to write it down, I didn't give it much thought. After all, I had had friends suggesting me to write on other issues on various earlier occasions too, but I always thought this was a task for the elderly who didn't face the rigours of a daily job.

In the meantime, Col Prasad Shrikant Purohit, a serving, decorated army officer had just been granted bail. His was a classic case as Purohit had become the face of this so-called Hindu terror all over the world. I made my first effort months after he came out on bail. Of course, the book materialised long after that. But at least the idea had germinated in my mind. Rather, I had become positively disposed towards Renu's idea.

The publisher is the best judge when it comes to the timeline but I am sure I took at least ten times more than the required duration to put together the whole story. The legwork to procure the documents and copies and talking to the right people alone took more than two years. On top of that came the travel and health restrictions owing to COVID. Suffice it to say that Renu, my friend and publisher, in that order, displayed exemplary patience. I do not know if she does the same with all her authors or the privilege was reserved for me.

We all keep hearing from the wise ones that often, the journey is the destination. For the first time in my life, I realised the depth of this philosophy. When I was finally informed that it is time to close the writing and we are ready for it, I felt a tinge of loss and emptiness. It was like writing this book had become a journey in self-exploration. I was cherishing the writing, the deleting, the thinking and the re-thinking. And in the process I had almost forgotten that this has to come out in concrete form one day.

As I write these last few lines, I have only gratitude for everyone whom I met and spoke to with regard to the incidents and investigations. Renu Kaul Verma, more than anyone else, for prodding me and reminding me constantly that this had to be done. Col Purohit who was initially reluctant but at least did not stop me from going ahead. Aparna Purohit, a woman of steel if ever there was one, for sharing her innermost thoughts and reliving all the pain just to give me the true picture.

Vinay Kumar, my esteemed colleague and the perfect back-room boy, a master of quick research and a repository of information on anything and everything. He is my walking encyclopaedia and friend of many years.

Kanagam and Alisha for their mellifluous expression, sharp eye for detail and for just being there at any time of the day and night whenever I required. Both these amazing women have convinced me that the finicky, strict and argumentative sub-editors in the news room are actually no match when it comes to book editors. More power to you girls.

RVS Mani, a man who is known to speak his mind, for filling me up wherever I faltered on the details and for never throwing any airs no matter how demanding I sometimes became.

Alas, a long list of persons without whom this book would not have been possible must remain unnamed and unrecorded. They are the real sources who guided me through the maze of information and helped me see things more clearly. Each of them will remain in my heart for their prompt co-operation, deep knowledge and commitment to the nation. I salute them without being able to name them here.

First Day, First Meet

It was a sunny but pleasant autumn morning. I had just landed at the domestic airport in Mumbai. The gust of humid air brought a tinge of irritation as my body had become accustomed to the dry North-Indian air ever since we moved out from Assam a few decades ago. More than a dozen worries played on my mind as I dragged my bag out onto the drive, the foremost being the impact of the flight delay on my schedule for the day.

I was in Mumbai to meet someone I had been trying to meet for more than seven years. Our common contacts had warned me that the gentleman was such a stickler for punctuality that he might cancel the meet if I was late even by a few minutes. And here I was, delayed by a late flight and a terrible jam just across the sea-link.

As I stepped into the small but spic and span twin-room official quarter of Lt Col Prasad Shrikant Purohit, what struck me at first glance was the mischievous half smile playing on the face of a wheatish complexioned, stocky, grey-eyed man. The eyes were, in fact, a strange mix of blue and grey, something I have only seen in *Punekars*[1]. I was looking at perhaps one of the most maligned, tortured and abused men I had ever met in my life. But there were also many who admired him, spoke highly of him and a few who unabashedly admitted that they idolised him. Now this was a strange package and something I had earlier associated only with politicians. The name that immediately comes to mind is of course Narendra Modi who invited similar extreme reactions since his days as the Chief Minister of Gujarat.

But then politicians are a different breed altogether. Here I was looking at a serving army officer, a salaried man. And also a man (I was to learn after several visits to Mumbai and countless conversations) who had nothing but the desire to do an honest day's work before going to bed at night; a man whose ambition was never to lead but just to serve; to serve his institution, the Indian Army, which had provided him the opportunity to do what other professions could not; the opportunity to serve his

---

1 *Punekars*: inhabitant or native of Pune

Motherland to whom he owed his very life breath, to serve the nation by remaining nameless, faceless, even perhaps place-less. Destiny had other things in store for him.

I could sense in his curt *namaskar* (traditional Indian greeting or gesture of respect) and stiff body language that Purohit was not very pleased to see me. He was certainly courteous as all officers are trained to be, but questions lurking in his mind cast a shadow on his brow which even a poor mind reader like me could not help noticing. I was to learn later, in the course of our long conversations, that the stiff body language was in fact second nature to him. Perhaps a reflection of the intelligence officer's training.

My reporter's instinct of putting the source at ease came in handy. I deliberately took out my cell phone from my shoulder bag and asked him whether he would feel happy if I kept it switched off during our conversation. This small (on the spur-of-the-moment) query from me became that essential ice-breaker we both needed badly. He looked at me for a couple of seconds, and then said it would make him feel much better if I did. It not only eased out his furrowed brow but brought a disarming smile to his face. From then on he relaxed and the conversation became easier and even faster.

Meanwhile, a *sahayak*-like (aide) person served us some patties and sweets. When I enquired if the patties were vegetarian, my host was quick to add, 'Madam, I saw Mishra in your name, and so I have ordered only vegetarian snacks today.' This was not something I had expected, and I decided not to tell him that most Mishras from Bihar relish non-vegetarian food including most members in my own extended family.

It was obvious that my host was trying to weigh me up. And therefore, not quite interested in engaging with me on the 'real issue' too soon. He was trying to make small talk by asking me what was going on in national politics, but here too he seemed to be more updated than I was. While I was mostly on what was going on in the capital's political circles and who was doing what, my host (without appearing to put any extra efforts) was telling me what would and could happen in the days to come. Whether he could do this owing to his sharp analytical skills or was privy to the 'right kind' of information, I cannot say. However, the situation wasn't very flattering for me, and I decided to come to what diplomats refer to as 'more substantive issues'. Enough of the small talk. Since there had been a court hearing in the Bombay High Court just a couple of days before my trip, I naturally referred to the last hearing first. He explained that things were moving ahead, though at a snail's pace. With MCOCA (Maharashtra Control of Organised Crime Act) removed, he was now totally focused on quashing the UAPA (Unlawful Activities (Prevention) Act) charge against him. The NIA (National Investigation Agency) had opposed the petition on various grounds. In a couple of sentences, Lt Col Purohit underlined the actual status of the case in the Bombay High Court. He also tried to explain to me, very briefly, the legal options available to him in the days to come.

The upshot of the whole conversation was that the prosecution had until then failed to prove the connecting link of Purohit with the men who were found involved in the blast at Malegaon. Purohit's claim was that nowhere did the charge-sheet establish beyond doubt that he had anything to do with those men. This was just the beginning of long months of conversation and research for me which started over a cup of coffee and patties at the spic and span two-room quarters of the officer.

While I still had to go through the piles and piles of court papers, I knew from my past field work that this man, who had literally been made the face of Hindu terror in the country and abroad, had a long story to tell. But the details of the case and its progress over the years had to wait. The man had been out of jail only recently, and I wanted to know whether and how he was picking up the threads of his life after those nine long nightmare years.

Yogic Positivity

One thing that struck me from the moment I met this man on the verandah of his two-room quarter was the glow of positivity on his face. This did not mean he was smiling a lot or laughing out loud. In fact, he maintained a pretty serious countenance most of the time. And was a focused, earnest kind of talker. It was just a strange calmness which was vividly noticeable at first glance. Or perhaps, I found it noticeable for the simple reason that what I saw on his face was totally contrary to what I had expected on the face of a man in his situation. If anything, I thought I would meet a person full of complaints for the politics of the country, perhaps abusing his fate (as we Indians find it easiest to do), definitely bad mouthing the agencies and perhaps even the judiciary or maybe the whole world at large. That is why the calmness on his face struck me as almost Yogic.

Of course, he had issues with the investigation, the judiciary, the agencies and the governments but the manner in which he discussed them was so professional, even clinical, that I felt he was discussing someone else's life with me. Whether clinical objectivity of looking at things was an intrinsic part of his character or the result of his training as a military intelligence officer or he had acquired it in jail post Malegaon was something I still needed to understand. Most likely, it was all these put together.

There was something else I found really strange and almost admirable. By piecing together the developments, I knew long before I met Purohit that a major part of his troubles lay in some bitter internecine conflict within his force. And yet every other sentence he uttered was full of praise for the faith, the support and the help being extended to him from the army's establishment. His words about the army reflected almost a kind of worship. Even after all that had happened, he was certain that the army could do no wrong even if he may have been wronged. From expecting to meet a guy, who was at best cynical and angry, or at worst bitter and broken; I had quite a surprise package here.

Even as I discerned an unwillingness on his part to go into the details of the case, I tried to steer the conversation to his chances of getting the UAPA charge quashed. He repeated a couple of times that he had enough documents at his disposal which would establish beyond doubt that he had nothing to do with the people who engineered the blast. He also claimed that he had documentary support to show that whatever activities he had done (as an undercover operative) was all in his official capacity as an officer of the intelligence network.

He even claimed that in private conversation, officers of the agencies, who were prosecuting him (mainly NIA), admitted that if all the documents were placed before the court, it would be difficult to hold the charges against him. Whether this claim was exaggerated or not, I would find time to check later, but one thing was certain: for a man facing charges of terror in a court of law and having spent years in jail, he exuded an unbelievable level of optimism which was almost amusing, since it appeared to me that the case didn't seem to be progressing much in his favour until then. And this was the most fascinating part of my memorable meeting.

Here was a man who could and should have been Indian's most bitter citizen considering the paradoxes of his life – a decorated army officer serving in the intelligence network to weed out the enemies of the nation, a die-hard patriot, who thought nothing of putting his own life in danger if it could help the establishment catch those who were plotting against the country, was himself the face of terror. And this terror was defined in the name of his religion. Hindu terror and Purohit were two terms being used synonymously for years in the media and in politics. While his wife ran from pillar to post for years seeking justice for her husband, his sons had grown up not only in his absence but with the stigma of being children of a terror accused.

Army Walon Ka Koi Nahi Hota

If the papers appeared to be in order, if the case file really did not establish his association with the persons who engineered the blast, and if his seniors in the army had vouched for him in black and white, what was taking things from coming back on track, I queried.

'Madam, *Army walon ka koi nahi hota*[2]!' he replied. Not sadly, not angrily but with a twinkling half-smile

---

2 *Army walon ka koi nahi hota:* people in the army have no one

which baffled me for weeks after my return from Mumbai.

I was left alone with my thoughts for some minutes as my host went into the balcony to attend to an urgent phone call. I took the liberty of strolling around his residence. Besides some essential furniture, the room had a small puja corner. In front of the Gods, lay a large prayer *mala* (prayer beads). The manner in which the mala had been kept on a piece of cloth indicated that it was used daily and maybe more than once.

The other room had a small pantry, not much cooking done there I could gather, a small dining table, a book shelf which had a curious collection of security/strategy related books and spiritual literature. The wall opposite to the book rack was lined with another wooden shelf with a glass pane displaying his favourite drinks. And pretty well-stocked, I thought.

A Tin Shed and the Two Loves

I had gone to my first meeting with Lt Col Prasad Shrikant Purohit with an apprehension that our *parichay* (association) would not continue beyond this first meeting. I had my reasons for thinking that way. Just because he agreed to see me owing to some common contacts did not necessarily mean he would be interested in discussing details. And, in fact, he didn't. However, he expressed his willingness to continue the association, to talk to me whenever possible and look me up if and when he travelled to Delhi. For me, this indication of not ending the association after the first meeting was good enough. Emboldened by the conversation, I asked him if he had ever thought of penning down the course of events post Malegaon. He replied in the affirmative. 'I am doing it for my sons,' he confided. The idea came to his mind one day, he said, when he thought what would happen if he never came out of jail. Would his sons be made to suffer all their lives? Would they be condemned to live forever with the stigma as their father languished within the prison walls? It was at that stage, he claimed, that he decided to put down in black and white all that had happened to him, and that was how he started writing it long hand in the prison cell. Day-by-day, night-by-night account of what had transpired all these years, starting long before the Malegaon blast but without divulging any security secrets.

Needless to say, I was intrigued and wanted to know if he would let me read them. He didn't say no, but then did not make any commitment either. Instead, he said he wanted to show me something else. I was expecting it to be some documents or writings which may throw some light on his case.

But he led me downstairs instead, towards the open courtyard. In a tin shed, at the far end of the courtyard, was a sleek, black/grey motorcycle covered partially by a canvas cloth. When he took off the cover, I held my breath. 'This is what I love,' he beckoned. As I looked more closely, I realised the bike was manufactured in Great Britain. 'It's the last batch of Enfield Bullet motorcycles sent from England before India started production here,' he claimed. There was a pride in his voice I had not felt during our entire conversation until then. Literally wiping a speck of dust from the front of the bike, he reminisced how he had cajoled and convinced a Commanding Officer early in life to sell him this bike, and the CO had parted with it almost as if he was losing a family member.

This was a different Purohit I was seeing, one who had passion and even love in his voice. But there was more to come. As I was trying to turn back towards the building and escape the blinding Sun, he pointed me towards the other end of the garage. 'You have not seen my other love,' he quipped. As I turned to follow his gaze, my eyes fell upon an open air jeep with all the old world charm one could imagine. Exactly the '*mere sapnon ki rani*[3]' variety. Maybe this was one of those things which kept the owner occupied and thus distracted him from thinking too much about his past, present and future. But was it really in running condition? I think the question came as an affront to my host and he almost took it as a

---

3   *mere sapnon ki rani*: reference to a popular Bollywood song where the hero drives a similar jeep

challenge. He sent a staffer immediately to get the keys and I got this short but terrific joy ride in his open jeep around the busy streets of Colaba. As the wind caught my hair, I could feel all the stress I had felt prior to our meeting and the intense conversation indoors dissipate. I closed my eyes and felt a strange calm, an unexplained stillness amidst the cacophony of the jeep whirring, the loud car horns, the pedestrians' noises.

As I flew back to Delhi, reminiscing over my brief but very interesting meeting with Lt Col Purohit, it struck me that despite so much being published in the newspapers in India and even abroad, there was perhaps not a single person outside a closed circle who really 'knew' the story of Malegaon or even what became known as Hindu/Saffron terror. Would people ever know? Or would this just die down and go out of public discourse after the occasional headlines in few city pages following court hearings? Wasn't it time to find out more about the incident which became the precursor to one of India's most polarised political debates, the debate over whether or not there was such a thing as Hindu terror.

If Purohit was made the face of Hindu terror, why was it him and not someone else? If this was a political conspiracy, who was it directed against and why? How would it help the conspirators? This and many more questions, which had troubled so many of us few years ago, came flooding back to my mind.

Recalling the advice of old-school editors that no piece of information is too small or irrelevant, I decided to start with whatever little I had in hand. But it took me several more months to really start any substantial work on the subject. In fact, most people I approached seemed to have lost interest in the case altogether. The National Investigation Agency (NIA), the federal agency which had taken charge of the case from the Maharashtra state Anti-Terror Squad (ATS), was too occupied with other cases it had started working on in recent years. Of these, the most engrossing was the labyrinthine terror funding cases. A casual conversation at NIA headquarters confirmed that the top brass had little interest left in the Malegaon blast case or the other so-called Hindu terror files. They gave the impression of having 'moved on' to more 'current' issues.

In the Malegaon case, there had been one more headline-grabbing development. Sadhvi Pragya Thakur, a saffron-clad student activist who was an accused in the case, had contested and handsomely won the Parliamentary election from Bhopal in 2019.

In public memory too, the Hindu terror cases were being referred to as something that was now part of history and to be discussed as a closed chapter. The atmosphere in the courts, however, did not reflect much optimism. After the filing of charge-sheets, the regular hearings in the Malegaon case continued to move at a snail's pace with most hearings getting adjourned without any development worth reporting at all. In the Bombay High Court, there were parallel hearings on the quashing of UAPA following the petition filed by Purohit and few others.

I decided I wanted to know more about the story than what had been told to us in the newspapers. With enough evidence in the public domain pointing towards the fact that Hindu terror was a political conspiracy of a much higher level than simple folks could ever imagine, I thought I would have done at least one satisfying task in life if even a single citizen (besides me) would feel convinced by what I found. And even if I failed to convince anybody, I owed it to the guy I had met on that humid Mumbai afternoon whose patriotism and concern for the security of the nation far outweighed his worries about his own life and future.

The Second Visit

When I boarded the plane back to Delhi after my first meeting with Purohit, I tried to impress upon myself that my trip to the seaside metropolis had been a fruitful one. On the contrary, the visit had left me anything but satisfied. It triggered a chain of thought which would not let me relax for weeks. After going over our conversation again and again in my mind, I booked another set of return tickets. However, this time I had a longer trip in mind and definitely a longer conversation. I also had a somewhat concrete proposal which I wanted to put on the table.

Immediately after I handed him his box of *Balushahi*[4] (everybody who knows Purohit is aware of his sweet tooth), I told him that it was time for facts to come out, that this book had to be written, and he should in no way put a spanner on my plans. He was silent for a few seconds, gave me a stern look, but then softly smiled and said I could go ahead.

Once I had obtained this crucial 'in principle' go-ahead, my mind felt easier. The tautness I had sensed in my muscles the whole day seemed to be loosening, and I was able to indulge in small talk over dinner. A strong sea-breeze lashed at us compelling us to raise our voices just to be heard across the dinner table. In Delhi, the breeze would have qualified as a storm, but *Mumbaikars*[5] dining around us didn't even seem to notice.

I boarded a flight back to Delhi with something new to look forward to. However, the relief was just too short-lived, as has always been the case with me in life. I had just landed and barely looked up at the night sky when I got a call from Purohit. Something tensed inside me.

4   *Balushahi*: A traditional Indian dessert prepared with all purpose flour, deep fried and soaked in sugar syrup
5   *Mumbaikars*: an inhabitant or native of Mumbai

Probably he was just checking if I had landed on time, I tried to convince myself. But of course it wasn't that. My subject had just given a curt notice that while there was no in-principle objection to writing, I should not expect any details related to the case except those already in the public domain. Nor should I expect him to share any case-related documents possessed by him or his associates. 'But that's crazy!! I can't write on hearsay. I must have substantial documentary support.' 'I am sorry Madam, you will have to manage with your reporting skills and resources to procure the necessary documentary support. The courts won't allow,' he told me rather bluntly. 'But the courts haven't proved anything yet in all these years,' I retorted. 'Whatever it is, these are my words,' he said and hung up. I was exasperated for some minutes but began to understand his point eventually.

Even after this 'fruitful' second trip, my work would not begin for months, but at least I had a task in hand, even if there was no deadline. And this was a task assigned to me by myself. I had to do it with my mind and heart even if it took forever.

It's Hindu Terror! Nation Stunned As Headlines Scream Hindu Terror

Lt Col Arrested for Malegaon Blast

'The Mumbai police arrested a serving Lt Col for allegedly supplying arms and explosives for the September 29 Malegaon blast. This is the first instance of an army officer being held in connection with a terror attack.'

This was reported by the prestigious pink daily *Economic Times* on the morning of 7 November 2008. Mumbaikars and Indians everywhere else woke up to almost identical headlines. The incident in reference was a blast that occurred on 29 September 2008 just outside the Hamidia Masjid in Malegaon killing six and injuring over a hundred people in the communally sensitive textile town. Lt Col Prasad Shrikant Purohit, a military intelligence officer, was at that time on a training course in Pachmarhi while his regular posting was at Deolali in Nashik.

But the shock of this initial headline paled before the vivid details that started trickling in at a surprising pace in India's various newspapers and magazines. Almost every day, there were 'stories' about how the serving army officer had floated a radical Hindu outfit and started building up a team by fanning sentiments against Islamic organisations and invoking Maratha pride. And then, how he had chosen an opportune time, when the faithful would be coming out of prayers, to trigger the blast. Purohit and his co-conspirators were accused of planning the attack, arranging the explosives and arms, and then sending them to a group of locals for planting at the site.

This was officially the start of a series of terror attacks branded as Hindu and Saffron terror by the government of the day, the police, our anti-terror agencies and the media. The subject was such that it was bound to find widespread resonance and it did. In a matter of few weeks, Hindu terror was 'the' hot topic in publications and debating circles in many countries. Security agencies and experts in various countries started writing commentaries and building up a whole new set of theories. We will check out some of them later.

Closer home, people professing the *Sanatana*[6] or the Hindu faith have been found to indulge in small and large-scale violence in various parts of the country during the post-1947 time period. From the partition-provoked riots to Nellie, 1984 anti-Sikh massacres and numerous political 'movements' of caste, language, regional and sub-national identities, rioting, arson and killings have been witnessed all across India. However, none of the violent incidents were defined or identified as Hindu terror regardless of the scale of violence.

Sources tell me the first known use of the term Saffron Terror appeared in a *Frontline* magazine article in 2002 in the context of the post-Godhra riots in Gujarat. But the term actually gained currency only after the Anti-Terror Squad in Maharashtra picked up Purohit. Briefings by ATS officers and media stories based on 'sources' claimed that Purohit, along with a group of radicalised, extremist *Hinduvaadi*[7] operatives, wanted to punish Muslims and this blast was just one of a series of many such attacks they had conspired. Some media reports also went on to say that Purohit and his associates such as Ramesh Upadhyaya (also an army personnel),

---

6   *Sanatana*: Sanatana dharma meaning 'eternal dharma' is an endonym used by Hindus to refer to Hinduism
7   *Hinduvaadi*: a person who follows Hinduism

Sadhvi Pragya Singh, Ramji Kalsangra were espousing a plan for a utopian Hindu Nation with its saffron flag and a separate constitution. More than a decade later, all these stories have remained just that…stories.

Samjhauta Express Blast

A bomb attack on 18 February 2007 in the Indo-Pak Samjhauta Express train led to heightened tensions between the two neighbours. The bomb blast, just few minutes short of midnight, occurred soon after the train had crossed Diwana near Panipat. It killed sixty-eight persons, of which forty-three were Pakistani nationals. The terror attack was immediately viewed as a brazen attempt to foil efforts towards improving of relations between New Delhi and Islamabad as Pakistan Foreign Minister Khurshid Mahmud Kasuri was scheduled to arrive in India just a day later.

For decades, the Samjhauta Express, started in 1976, was the only train service between the two countries, till Thar Express was launched with the special efforts of Jaswant Singh.

For long months, agencies investigating the blast held that the main accused Arif Qasmani, a Pakistani national, was responsible for triggering the attack. Ace reporter on internal security, Vicky Nanjappa (then working for Rediff.com), writes that when the investigation began, top SIMI (Students' Islamic Movement of India) operative

Safdar Nagori had told the agencies that 'the attack was carried out by the members of his outfit' along with help from Lashkar-e-Taiba. Arif Qasmani had played a pivotal role in arranging the finances and other logistics for the attack. The theory was corroborated almost to the word by US investigating agencies probing into Pakistan's terror network.

But when the NIA took over the investigation in 2010, the SIMI probe went cold and Samjhauta blast was billed as a conspiracy by Hindu extremists led by 'mastermind' Swami Aseemanand (earlier Naba Kumar Sarkar) and others. They were charge-sheeted by NIA in 2011. Later, in 2016, Aseemanand was given bail for lack of evidence.

Though never named as an accused in the case, Col Purohit's name was mentioned in sources-based news stories on the Samjhauta blast referring to it as part of the larger Hindu terror conspiracy. It was claimed that the provocation for attacking the Samjhauta Express was to derail any peace talks and overtures between the Indian and Pakistani governments.

Ajmer Sharif Blast

Ajmer Sharif blast, one of the four other terror incidents labelled as Hindu terror, occurred on 11 October 2007, just a few days short of Eid. It was sunset time, and the faithful had just started gathering for *Iftar*[8]. The blast was triggered in the courtyard of Khwaja Moinuddin Chishti Dargah, one of the holiest shrines for Muslims in India but also frequented by Hindus and Sikhs in huge numbers. Two persons were killed and seventeen injured by the bomb placed in a tiffin carrier. As in all other such incidents, the primary investigation focused on Pakistan-based Lashkar-e-Taiba through their operatives in India, but it was later billed as the handiwork of Hindu extremists.

Mecca Masjid Blast

The Mecca Masjid blast on 18 May 2007 was another sensational terror attack of the same year. Nine persons were killed in the blast during Friday prayers and sixty-odd were injured. However, five more got killed in police firing as violence broke out in the area immediately after the blast.

The case is considered closed now as all five accused were let off in April 2018 for lack of evidence.

The Same Story

Some glaring points stand out in the investigations of all these cases. That they were the work of Hindu extremist

---

8   *Iftar*: The evening meal with which Muslims end their daily Ramadan fast at sunset

groups. That it was only one set of people who planned all the attacks. That Abhinav Bharat, a militant Hindu group, was instrumental in bringing them together and organising the logistics for the attack. That in almost all the cases, there was hardly any variation in the list of accused, which included names such as Swami Aseemanand, Ramchandra Kalsangra, Devendra Gupta, Sandeep Dange, Sunil Joshi, Lokesh Sharma, Sadhvi Pragya Thakur, Bharat Mohanlal or Bharat Bhai and so on.

Of these, Lt Col Purohit was accused only in the Malegaon blast, though his name did crop up briefly in the Samjhauta context. But for reasons never explained in so many words (yet obvious), it was the uniformed soldier who would be portrayed in the media and political circles as the face of Hindu terror in India.

The Other Malegaon Blasts

More than two years prior to the Hamidia Masjid blast in Malegaon for which Col Purohit was arrested by the ATS, a series of blasts rocked the small but communally sensitive town on 8 September 2006. These blasts claimed forty lives and more than a hundred were injured. The aftermath of the blast was completely baffling as the 'sources' pointed at Pakistan sponsored operatives, SIMI, the Sangh Parivar outfit Bajrang Dal and Abhinav Bharat – all at the same time. It was like the agencies were deliberately creating a maze of theories, or they were genuinely befuddled about the real story of the attack. Eventually, the investigation was taken over by NIA and the suspicion centred on Abhinav Bharat. A court in 2016 dropped the MCOCA charges against all those accused who had been arrested by the ATS initially in 2006.

Netas Beat Each Other in Demonising Saffron

We will come back to the trajectory the investigations took in the course of the following chapters. However, police investigations (even those pertaining to terror attacks) tend to run into decades. Added to this is the inordinate delay in the courts of law with dozens of hearings closing without even a word of progress in the case. But the investigations into the purported Hindu terror cases started playing out simultaneously at the political level as well. It opened the floodgates for political statements, allegations and conspiracy theories like never before. During the years when the investigations into the cases were the 'talk of the town', it almost appeared as if *netas*[9] were participating in a contest to beat each other in issuing statements and tweets establishing the horror of Hindu terror. While these statements were coming out with unusual frequency (often several times a week), some of them have 'stood the test of time' and are quoted till date.

---

9   *netas*: politicians or leaders of an organisation

Of them, the most frequent and often most diabolic were the comments of senior Congress leader Digvijay Singh. His remarks on Hindu terror or RSS terror, as he liked to qualify, were provocative and therefore elicited the predictable reactions among RSS and its supporters. But despite being one of the most quoted leaders of his party on this subject, Singh was not part of the government. His statements could thus be taken as the views of a politician fighting the political war against his ideological opponents. What really caused concern, debate and invited international attention were the statements of top government functionaries, including successive Home Ministers. It created serious unease in the internal security quarters. What was more embarrassing was the opportunity it provided our neighbour, Pakistan, to draw an 'equivalence' with India on the issue of terror. It gave our neighbour, and many within India, the chance to shift the focus at a crucial stage when undivided attention was needed to expose Pakistan following the horrific Mumbai attack.

Here I am quoting just a few of those which need to be kept in perspective if the entire phenomenon of Hindu terror is to be understood by the country, particularly, by observers like me who have always been baffled by its sudden appearance on the horizon.

Setting aside party voices such as Digvijay Singh for the moment, I want to highlight a telling statement of the then Union Home Minister P Chidambaram on 25 August 2010.

'I wish to caution you that there is no let-up in the attempts to infiltrate militants into India. There is no let-up in the attempts to radicalise young men and women in India. Besides, there is the recently uncovered phenomenon of "saffron terrorism" that has been implicated in many bomb blasts of the past....'

A few years later, another senior Congress leader Sushil Kumar Shinde, who succeeded Chidambaram as the Home Minister went further and accused the RSS of 'conducting terror training' for spreading 'saffron terrorism'.

Shinde once said,

'This has come so many times in the papers...It is not a new thing that I have said today. This is the saffron terrorism that I have talked about. It is the same thing and nothing new. It has come in the media several times.'

On the same day, while answering a query on the issue, Shinde said, 'This is (the) saffron terrorism (that) I have stated.' But there was expected furore on the term following which Home Minister Sushil Kumar Shinde issued a clarification of sorts. He said,

'It has been understood to mean that I was linking terrorism to a particular religion and was accusing certain political organisations of being involved in organising terror camps. I had no intention to link terror to any religion...since a controversy has been created on account of my statement, I am issuing this clarification and expressing regret to those who felt hurt by my statement.'

Shinde had made these statements in the months of January and February 2013 during a party conclave in Jaipur and other occasions. Notwithstanding the minister's clarification, RK Singh, the then Union Home Secretary said on 22 January 2013 that at least ten people having close links with the Rashtriya Swayamsevak Sangh (RSS) and its affiliated organisations were named accused in various acts of terror. Singh said,

'Yes, during investigations of Samjhauta Express, Mecca Masjid and Ajmer Dargah Sharif blasts, we have found names of at least ten persons who have been associated with the RSS at some point or the other.... We have evidence against them... there are statements of witnesses.'

Singh's words would come back to haunt him later when he joined the BJP and became a minister in 2014 in the Narendra Modi government. Netizens active on social media networks did not fail to remind him of his old remarks for many months. Since then, much water has flown under the bridge, and RK Singh continues to hold charge of important portfolios in the centre as one of the better performing ministers.

As stated above, if there was one person who kept on a relentless tirade against the RSS in the name of Hindu terror, it was veteran Congressman and two-time Chief Minister of Madhya Pradesh, Digvijay Singh. Since Singh issued statements every other day on some conspiracy angle or other, it is exhaustive to quote all of them here. But when he was accused of using Hindu terror too often, he replied once that he only mentioned 'Sanghi terrorism' and that he had never coined Hindu terrorism.

Of the statements which have remained in public consciousness for a very long time, and still get quoted whenever the subject of Hindu terror is touched upon, the remarks made by then Congress leader and later party President (now resigned) Rahul Gandhi deserve mention here. A WikiLeaks cable claimed Rahul Gandhi had said in 2009 that although 'there was evidence of some support for the group (Islamic terrorist group Lashkar-e-Taiba) among certain elements in India's indigenous Muslim community, the bigger threat may be the growth of radicalised Hindu groups, which create religious tensions and political confrontations with the Muslim community'.

Since the leaked remarks were made during a conversation with the US envoy in India, Timothy Roemer, it cannot be sufficiently underscored how damaging this statement was for India's image abroad and the perception it created in the international world.

This statement, which came out of the WikiLeaks expose, would haunt the Congress leadership, particularly the Nehru Gandhi scion, for long years to come. It led to a furore in Parliament the very morning the story hit the headlines, and BJP leaders Sushma Swaraj, Arun Jaitley, Rajnath Singh along with others led the charge in both the Lok Sabha and Rajya Sabha demanding an apology from the Congress party as well as the government. But the protests did not end there. In fact, the statement would serve as cannon fodder for a long time to come. Every time Rahul Gandhi frequented a temple or Hindu shrine in the course of his election campaigns, the BJP leaders and their army of internet supporters would waste no time in reminding him of his leaked conversation with the US envoy Roemer.

Expectedly, the political slugfest between BJP and Congress over these statements from Chidambaram to Digvijay to Shinde would play out episodically every few months and definitely when there were elections around. Supporters would adopt strident positions depending on which side they leaned towards. Digital warriors would take digs at each other but sometimes snap at leaders of their own sides too. For instance, the BJP leaders would often be confronted by their own supporters on social media platforms for not doing enough to help those who were caught in the conspiracy and were suffering as under-trials in jails or undergoing hardships due to unending court cases. I have already mentioned how the so-called right-wing netizens and social media army came out with some really uncharitable comments on RK Singh.

On the other hand, the likes of Digvijay Singh, who were seen as relentlessly reminding the country of Hindu terror, were plastered by their own party men for derailing the Congress party's focus on other issues and in turn giving their rivals a chance to consolidate the Hindus.

Politics over Hindu terror has been around for more than a decade now, so we shall come to that again and again in the ensuing chapters.

Hindu Terror – a Godsend for Pakistan

More sinister and much more damaging than the domestic political battle was the fact that Hindu terror became not just a potent weapon but a Godsend for Pakistan to point fingers at us whenever it was called out for exporting terror to India. From the horrific Mumbai attacks to Samjhauta Express blasts, Pakistan did its best to mount the high horse, and tried telling the international powers that these attacks were India's own doing and that accusing Pakistan was nothing but a fabrication. It did not stop at that. Some elements in Pakistan, proscribed internationally as terrorists, even demanded that India be declared a terrorist state. Not that the world took it seriously, but it did lead to a false equalising of sorts on the most important issue of global terror. This, in turn, weakened our arguments and pushed us into a defensive position more than once in the international arena. Sample this:

An *Indian Express* report on 21 January 2013:

> Mumbai attacks mastermind and LeT founder Hafiz Saeed sought to exploit Home Minister Sushil Kumar Shinde's jibe against RSS and BJP saying Indian 'propaganda' against Pakistani organisations of spreading terror now stood 'exposed'. ...he went to the extent of levelling an accusation that Indian organisations were 'involved in all kinds of terrorism in Pakistan'.

Where Saeed stands in the terror world is no secret. There could not be a bigger irony than Hafiz Saeed accusing India of spreading terror. So I move on to what some people, including observers and experts on internal security, had to say.

Of course, politicians in Pakistan lapped it up. The then principal opposition party Pakistan Tehreek-e-Insaf (PTI) leader Shafqat Mahmood, who was heading their information team, smugly remarked, 'Samjhauta Express is one example, but there are other instances that prove their involvement in massacres in both Gujarat and Mumbai.' By 'their' Mahmood meant Hindu terrorists of course.

The Indian Defence Review, a publication started in 1986 by a former Army captain and widely followed by all who are interested in the subject of internal and external security wrote this on 13 February 2012:

> The much touted success of the investigative agencies in linking the blasts in Samjhauta Express, Mecca Masjid and other blasts to 'Hindu terror' or 'Saffron terror' raises more questions than it answers.
>
> While vote-bank politics of some political outfits may have been served, India has lost. The police and the investigative agencies have been politicised and their credibility stands shattered. Even the newly formed National Investigation Agency (NIA) has been rendered vulnerable to political manipulation. The inspired leaks of Swami Aseemanand's confession and flip flops over it bear testimony.... As and when Pakistan unleashes the next terror attack on India, the Pakistan authorities will deny it and demand that it be first established whether it was 'Hindu terror' or 'Islamic terror'.

What a powerful handle was given to Pakistan, a country termed by our own diplomats as the epicentre of terror, can be gauged from the fact that even as recently as 29 September 2019, former Pakistan Prime Minister Imran Khan sought to exonerate his country of India's accusations by raising the same charges. He quoted figures of massacres of Muslims in various parts of the country and the rendering of one and a half lakh Muslims homeless. And not surprisingly, the only support he furnished to buttress his claims were the statements of UPA ministers already quoted earlier in this chapter.

The damage that the Hindu terror narrative inflicted on New Delhi's fight against Pakistan and ISI-sponsored Jihadi terror was most clearly and emphatically brought out by ace diplomat, strategic affairs expert and former High Commissioner to Pakistan G Parthasarthy in his widely read article, 'Pak let off the hook on 26/11' published on 17 February 2011. Parthasarthy wrote,

> India received unprecedented international support to deal with the perpetrators of 26/11. The Israelis have filed a highly publicised law suit in a New York court against Lashkar chief, Hafiz Mohammed Saeed, and ISI boss Lt General Shuja Pasha for their role in the Mumbai attack. We have, however, shot ourselves in the foot, thanks to some divisive and irresponsible statements by some of our politicians, voicing concern about

'Hindu terrorism' in India.

The damage caused by these irresponsible statements became evident when I recently met a group of distinguished Pakistanis, who averred that India had no right to insist on action against the perpetrators of the 26/11 terrorist attack on Mumbai, as it had taken no action against the 'Hindu terrorists' responsible for the deaths of Pakistani nationals in the Samjhauta Express bomb blasts.

Parthasarthy further mentioned that Pakistan has also launched a campaign claiming that the Indian Army is full of 'Hindu terrorists' like Lt Col Shrikant (sic) Purohit, now under arrest, for involvement in the Malegaon blasts.

While concluding his column, Parthasarthy outlined the long-term fall-out of the developments: 'Irresponsible statements have resulted in India paying a high price internationally.'

Though there were any number of political columns written on the face-off between the ruling UPA (mainly Congress) and the opposition BJP, particularly during the latter half of UPA-II regime, I would like to quote just one more news story here.

This was a news analysis published in the web portal 'Samvad' by veteran journalist Pramod Kumar.

He mentions how then Home Minister Sushil Kumar Shinde's remarks on Hindu terror had been picked by terrorists like Hafiz Saeed and HuJI commander Ilyas Kashmiri across the border and led them to make the obnoxious demand that India be declared a 'terrorist state'. Kumar, quoting veteran parliamentarian and then Chairman of the prestigious Public Accounts Committee Dr Murli Manohar Joshi, wrote, 'Before linking saffron with terror, Shinde Saheb should know the significance of saffron colour in Indian life. It symbolises our identity and by linking it with terror, you have linked the entire nation with terrorism. You have insulted not only the age-old Hindu culture and traditions but also the entire nation.'

As per Pramod Kumar's story, Dr Joshi then went on to stress how a United Nations Security Council Committee on Sanctions had said, 'Arif Qasmani, chief co-ordinator of the Lashkar-e-Taiba had funded the Samjhauta Express blast, with the Al-Qaeda providing the staff for the blast.' Joshi had dealt in detail about the role of David Coleman Headley, his third wife Faiza Outalha and various SIMI top operatives in the blast.

And then Dr Joshi, pointedly blaming the NIA, said, 'These evidences demolish the entire story framed by the National Investigation Agency (NIA) on Samjhauta blast case….these facts destroy the case of the NIA and confirm the evil intent of the political establishment in the country,' thus voicing on the floor of the Parliament what RSS bigwigs had been alleging for a long time, that Hindu terror was a creation of the Congress leadership (heading the UPA government) with malicious political intent.

RSS and Hindu Terror

It was the fag end of 2008. Newspaper headlines were screaming Hindu terror every morning. Channels were airing special shows narrating how conspiracies were being hatched all over the country by fanatic Hindu extremists possessed by hate for Muslims and trying to shatter India's centuries-old culture of harmony. Most stories were 'source' based without much documentary evidence to support them. In the midst of all this, I called up an articulate RSS officer-bearer to know how exactly they were dealing with the crisis. He agreed to speak in detail on the condition that he not be quoted in my reports.

As we started, he tried to repeat the stock statements we had been reporting for months. But in about twenty minutes, he warmed up and moved away from the cases and names to the larger challenge that the organisation was faced with. He spoke how new revelations every day would force the top brass of the Sangh to keep 'explaining' about their organisation everywhere they went, in the country and abroad. He was worried about the morale of the *swayamsevaks* (volunteers) who displayed blind faith in the organisation. He also pointed out that since the RSS did not have a system of formal membership, it was only this faith and attachment which kept the cadre going. His biggest worry was providing legal support to accused persons even as the RSS 'detached' itself from the people involved.

'Yes, this is a challenge which is reaching serious proportions now,' he admitted after few moments of pensive silence. 'How serious?' I persisted. 'Well, we have not faced anything more serious in terms of defamation and propaganda since the allegation about Mahatma Gandhi's assassination,' he candidly confessed. And then this otherwise talkative leader lapsed into silence. When he finally spoke again, there was a half-smile on his lips, and in a resolve-like manner he said that just like the allegation in 1948 was fought and contested, this too would be fought, contested, challenged with equal if not greater vigour. He also pointed out that this time round it could be a much bigger challenge than even 1948 because of the media, which had now expanded exponentially since the 1940s, and a world which was becoming increasingly intolerant towards terror since the 9/11 twin towers terror attack that shook everyone.

I came out of this RSS functionary's residence-cum-office with a strange feeling. On the one hand, there was resolve on his face displaying an amused kind of indulgence that such things were every-day challenges for the organisation which they had got used to contesting over decades. And just as earlier allegations and attacks could not stop their growth, even this one would come and go. On the other hand, there were moments during our conversation when I felt that there was a feeling of being hemmed in by a very fast developing chain of events which could threaten the reputation and hence the growth of the RSS.

Early the next morning, when my news story came out in the paper that I was serving then, the RSS leader called back to say that I had written a great copy; a compliment I had never received from anybody in that organisation.

Within few weeks of our meeting, names of more high-ranking RSS *pracharaks*[10] flashed in the headlines, sometimes from Uttar Pradesh, at other times from Rajasthan and Madhya Pradesh.

A predictable chain of events was becoming almost routine. First, names of a couple of senior RSS pracharaks or former RSS functionaries would flash in the headlines. In few cases, they were actually called for interrogation too. These copies would then lead to several follow-ups in which an 'association' would be established to indicate that these persons were operating with the

---

10 *pracharak*: A missionary or recruiter belonging to Rashtriya Swayamsevak Sangh

logistic, financial and moral support of the RSS top brass – starting with Ashok Berry and Ashok Varshneya to Indresh Kumar to finally the *sarsanghchalak* or the RSS chief Mohan Madhukarrao Bhagwat. While Indresh Kumar faced the heat for years, Berry and Varshneya were questioned but no cases made out.

Wild speculation and the lack of denial apart, here is a list of the persons, who were either RSS functionaries or had been swayamsevaks earlier, whose names cropped up in cases of Hindu terror. While some were let off after a few rounds of questioning or initial court hearing, many of them were charge-sheeted. A few later got acquitted, but several others are still fighting it out in the courts.

One morning in January 2013, several newspapers simultaneously published a list of RSS and former RSS persons claiming that they were all involved in a spate of terror attacks in the country. These stories were all attributed to the NIA. Here I am quoting one of the news reports. This is to indicate the general trend of stories those days. The others stories were also almost identical. The names and explanations attached have been reproduced exactly from the news copies.

> **Sunil Joshi:** RSS activist active in Dewas and
> Mhow from 1990s to 2003
> Involved in: Samjhauta and Ajmer Shrine blasts.
> Has died

Sandeep Dange: RSS pracharak active in Mhow, Indore, Uttarkashi and Sajhapur from 1990s to 2006

Involved in: Samjhauta, Mecca Masjid and Ajmer blasts.

On the run

Lokesh Sharma: RSS 'Nagar karyavahak' in Deogarh

Involved in: Samjhauta and Mecca Masjid blasts.

Was arrested

Swami Aseemanand: Was associated with RSS wing Vanavashi Kalyan Parishad in Dang, Gujarat, from 1990s to 2007

Involved in: Samjhauta, Mecca Masjid and Ajmer explosions.

Arrested

Rajender alias Samunder: Was RSS Varg Vistarak

Involved in: Samjhauta and Mecca Masjid blasts.

Arrested

Mukesh Vasani: Was an activist of RSS in Godhra, Gujarat

Involved in: Ajmer blast.

Arrested

Devender Gupta: RSS pracharak in Mhow and

Indore
Involved in: Mecca Masjid blast.
Arrested
Chandrasekhar Leve: RSS pracharak in
Shajhanpur in 2007
Involved in: Mecca Masjid blast.
Arrested
Kamal Chouhan: RSS pracharak
Involved in: Samjhauta and Mecca Masjid
explosions.
Arrested
Ramji Kalsangra: RSS associate.
Involved in: Samjhauta Express and Mecca
Masjid blasts.
On the run

The stories also gave an additional list which included
well-known and active RSS leaders.

1. **Indresh Kumar**, RSS
Linked to the blasts accused, probed for: Close
links with Sunil Joshi and Devender Gupta.
RSS national executive member and close
associate of Mohan Bhagwat, the sarsanghchalak,
one of the Sangh Parivar's main strategists. He
is alleged to have been the major force behind
communalising the Amarnath agitation in 2008

and also mobilising the Madhesis in Nepal against the Maoists. He launched the Muslim Ekta Manch to rally together 'nationalist' Muslims.

Investigating agencies are examining his links with Devendra Gupta, key accused in the 2007 Ajmer Sharif bombing. Also being probed are his ties with Sunil Joshi, suspected to be the bomber behind the Mecca Masjid and Ajmer Sharif blasts.

2. **Sunil Joshi**, RSS

Blast accused, whose murder is a mystery, accused of: Ajmer Sharif and Mecca Masjid bombings.

The main suspect in the 2007 blasts, this RSS pracharak was a friend of Malegaon accused Pragya Thakur and also faced the charge of murdering a local Congress leader. He was close to Swami Aseemanand, who had warned him of the imminent threat to his life post the blasts. Joshi had said to his friends that his mentor was Indresh Kumar. Investigating agencies are probing Joshi's hand in the Amritsar-Lahore Samjhauta Express blasts in February 2007.

3. **Devendra Gupta**, RSS

His mobile sim 'triggered' Ajmer blast, accused of: Mecca Masjid and Ajmer Sharif dargah blasts. An RSS pracharak with Abhinav Bharat links,

Gupta was arrested in Ajmer on April 28 on the charge of purchasing the SIM card that had triggered the Ajmer Sharif dargah bomb on October 11, 2007.

The SIM card had been purchased in Jharkhand, along with ten others.

Gupta is alleged to have been close to Sunil Joshi and Ramchandra Kalsangra, who had allegedly planted the bomb in Malegaon.

Gupta met Joshi in Mhow in 2006 and it was Kalsangra who introduced him to Pragya Thakur.

4. **Dayanand Pande**, RSS

Spiritual guru of Abhinav Bharat and porn purveyor, accused of: September 2008 Malegaon blast.

Born Sudhakar Udaybhan Dwivedi, he has taken on many names. He started life as Swami Amrutnand Devtirth and then took on the more pious-sounding title of Shankaracharya and settled in Kashmir.

All the terror meetings were held in his presence and all the accused addressed him as 'swamiji'. His habit of recording all meetings and saving them on his laptop proved to be his undoing. The recordings are being used as evidence against him and his cohorts. Apart from these audio and video clips, cops have also found a cache of obscene pictures and clips that he had downloaded from the Net.

5. **Major Ramesh Upadhyaya** (Retired)

ABHINAV BHARAT, stalker who talked of 'pure' Hindu Rashtra, accused of: September 2008 Malegaon blast.

Upadhyaya retired from the Army in 1988 and was the chief of the BJP's ex-servicemen's cell in Mumbai. The Maharashtra ATS claims he was a mere 'member' of the organisation, but from the tapes recovered from Pande, it seems he was present in all meetings where the Malegaon bombing was planned.

6. **Pragya Thakur**

Sannyasin with an unholy obsession with bloodshed, accused of: September 2008 Malegaon blast.

L.K. Advani might have defended her by claiming that she was a sadhvi but there was nothing holy about Pragya's thoughts and actions. Advani's claim was torn to shreds by the ATS, whose recorded telephone intercepts reveal how Pragya was disappointed when she heard that 'just three people' had been killed in the Malegaon. Her involvement in Abhinav Bharat's activities may not have been much, but she is suspected to have procured the explosives for the Malegaon blast. She didn't get along with Purohit as both claimed to be leaders of the 'Hindu Rashtra' movement.

7. **Shrikant P Purohit**, Lt Col, military intelligence arms procurer;
Gun-runner on the side, accused of: September 2008 Malegaon blast.

A fitness fanatic who knows four languages, the former Military Intelligence officer is said to be the brain behind the operation. The ATS believes Purohit had procured weapons and even RDX from an Army depot. Ironically, the man who wore Army colours is heard declaring in the Pande tapes that he doesn't believe in the Constitution. The ATS says he knows about the other blasts and the people who carried them out, but he refuses to talk. Purohit was not averse to making money on the side. He was into gun-running as well.

8. **Swami Aseemanand**
Mastermind and good friend of Gujarat Chief Minister Narendra Modi.
The ATS does not list him as an accused, but he's

very much under the scanner. The Kolkata native, known as Jatin Chatterjee before he donned his ochre robes, came to the Dangs district of Gujarat for a campaign to bring Christian converts back into the Hindu fold. A respected leader of the RSS, Aseemanand is said to be very close to Gujarat Chief Minister Narendra Modi, which may be why the ATS has not been able to catch up with him. His interrogation will provide the ATS clues to piece together the Hindutva terror jigsaw.

9. **Ramachandra Kalsangra** and **Sandeep Dange**
Suspected bombers, accused of: Malegaon, Mecca Masjid and Ajmer Sharif blasts.
Very little is known about these shadowy characters except that they're both from Indore and are suspected to be the bombers in the Malegaon, Mecca Masjid and Ajmer Sharif blasts. They've eluded the CBI, which has declared a reward of Rs 10 lakh on each of them. Dange is also known as Parmanand; Kalsangra's aliases are Ramji or Vishnu Patel. Both are around 35 years old and suspected to be major players in the Hindutva terror network.

10. **Ashok Varshney** and **Ashok Berry**, RSS
Linked to blasts, accused of: Providing assistance

to Devendra Gupta.

The two are being investigated by CBI for their alleged role in the Ajmer Sharif and Mecca Masjid blasts. Varshney, a former RSS prant pracharak in Jharkhand, had allegedly sourced and handed over two SIM cards to Devendra Gupta, a key accused in the Ajmer Sharif bombing.

11. **BL Sharma 'Prem'**, BJP

Planning big on the mass conversions of Muslims, accused of: One of Abhinav Bharat's founders. Close to Pandey and Purohit.

Also known as Prem Singh Sher after he embraced the Khalsa Panth in 1999, Sharma is a two-time BJP Member of the Lok Sabha. He was first elected from East Delhi in 1991 and then in 1996. He fought the last parliamentary elections in 2009 from Delhi North East, but lost to Jai Prakash Aggarwal.

12. **Rakesh Dhawade** and **Sharad Kunte**

Linked with bomb making, accused of: Dhawade, of imparting bomb training. He accuses Kunte of being engaged in the same task.

A research fellow at the Institute of Research and Development in Oriental Studies (IRDOS), Pune, Dhawade has been charged by the

Maharashtra ATS with "imparting training and exploding a bomb in Parbhani and Jalna". Dhawade is said to be a 'weapons collector' because of his vast collection of antique arms. In a statement recorded before a magistrate, Dhawade has named Sharad Kunte, a Pune professor who teaches at the Narsooji Wadia College, as the man who taught students to make bombs. Kunte was the VHP's Pune unit president for many years. He has been questioned by the ATS, but not booked.

13. **Lokesh Sharma**

Abhinav Bharat murder accused and blast suspect, accused of Involvement in the Ajmer Sharif bombing.

The Indore resident, who is among the 14 who have been charged with the murder of a local Congress leader in August 2003, was picked up by the Rajasthan ATS from the Chhindwara district of Madhya Pradesh on May 14. The ATS got wind of him after it had questioned the Ajmer blast accused, Devendra Gupta and Chandrashekhar Borad, who had been arrested on April 29. Sunil Joshi, deceased suspected bomber, was also one of the accused in the Congress leader's murder. Sharma is out on bail in the case. The common

link that binds all of them is their loyalty to the
fiery sadhvi, Pragya Thakur.

Around the same time that these names were 'released'
by the NIA, a sting operation was done by a group of
journalists and aired on a leading television channel. In
one part of the sting operation, the reporter is shown
talking to a 'witness'. The witness was said to be a close
associate of Sunil Joshi and had given his statement to
the ATS and CBI in which he had reportedly claimed
that senior RSS leader Indresh Kumar was 'aware' of the
terror plot and blast at Ajmer Sharif. However, look at
this conversation as shown in the sting....

Reporter: So Indresh was the driving force behind
Sunil Joshi's activities?

Witness: If you mentor someone and are his
godfather, it cannot be possible that you aren't
aware of his activities.

Reporter: And Joshi was very close to Indresh?

Witness: Yes, he used to claim so.

Reporter: He said he was always with him?

Witness: He would say that he was in constant
communication with Indreshji.

The purpose of quoting the above excerpt from
the sting is just to give an idea of the stories that were
appearing and the general drift of the entire narrative.

As obvious from the above excerpts, most of the theories relied on the logic of 'association' and what 'must have been' or 'could have been', rather than actual evidence or facts in hand.

Society Never Bought the Hindu Terror Story: Sangh

I have explained above the concern, the dilemma and the troubles that the RSS top leadership was going through when cases of purported Hindu terror were making headlines every morning. It is a fact of life that things always appear easier in hindsight. Perhaps the same applied to the RSS as well. But that should not prevent me from sharing with everyone here another very interesting conversation I had with one more top-ranking Sangh functionary who is also an ideologue and among the decision makers of the organisation.

I asked him the same question I had asked the previous leader in much the same words. That is, how serious was (or is) the challenge of Hindu terror for their organisation considering many of those charge-sheeted or let off were associated with the Sangh? He first reiterated what had been said in most of the RSS press statements already that those persons had not been in the Sangh when they were named in the cases though some of them may have had an old association.

But when I pointed out that the RSS as an organisation

had been accused of fomenting Hindu terror, he reacted sharply. Terming the accusation as nothing but fabrication, the RSS ideologue retorted that society had never, even for a moment, bought the theory. To buttress his claim, he cited some statistics. According to him, the RSS registered a jump of over 19000 *shakhas* (branches) during the 2010-2019 period. However, he pointed out that the rise in the shakhas was evenly distributed over the decade thus arguing that it did not coincide with the coming of Narendra Modi or a BJP-led government in the centre.

Now this was something I had to probe a little more. When I checked the data for the relevant period, I found that out of the 19000-odd shakhas, which were added between 2010-2019, around 13000 shakhas pertained to the period post Narendra Modi taking charge as Prime Minister in May 2014. This left us with a little more than 6000 shakhas in the UPA-II regime. On breaking it up further, it was clear that while 2000-odd shakhas were added every year during the Modi 1.0, it was an addition of just about 1000 shakhas during the previous regime. Now, while the latter figure may be just half of the Modi government tenure, we cannot gloss over the fact that even when Hindu terror was 'the' headline in the media and the biggest 'threat' as per the bigwigs in the then government, at least around 1000 shakhas were getting added every year. In other words, the RSS ideologue did have a point when he claimed that common citizens were not quite affected. At least, in as far as the RSS as an organisation was concerned, though they may have had doubts and questions about certain individuals.

This Sangh ideologue, who is also a master organiser, wasn't satisfied with just giving some data. He wanted to be more specific. So he narrated the example of a couple who are both Indian Police Service (IPS) officers. The couple, who had their roots in Deoria and Jaunpur districts of Uttar Pradesh, had served in various capacities in the state before joining the United Nations in some advisory capacities. The husband and wife had served separately in Jordan, Jerusalem and other conflict-ridden areas of the Middle-east gathering vast experience. 'But the goings-on back in India, especially the entire Hindu terror narrative jolted them so much that they decided to head home. Immediately after return, they met with a senior RSS functionary of Eastern UP and expressed their desire to join us as regular swayamsevaks and help us in whatever manner possible.'

The RSS leader's obvious claim in mentioning this couple's example was to drive home his argument that Hindu terror may have grabbed eyeballs in the media, both domestic and global, but it failed to raise any doubts, much less discredit the RSS in the minds of the common Hindu.

'We never felt the need to disprove the allegations in an organised manner at any stage,' he insisted. According to him, swayamsevaks had taken it upon themselves on individual initiative. However, he did mention one round of *dharnas* (sit-in protests) at all district headquarters. It was more to energise the cadre than anything else, he claimed. As for the legal challenges, he said the vast strength of lawyers, who are swayamsevaks, helped them deal with the court cases without any financial burden on the organisation.

Now here was something I could actually vouch for. When the RSS senior mentioned lawyers, I was immediately reminded of the late Arun Jaitley, whom I had witnessed poring over the various Hindu terror cases for long hours, at the time when the issue was at its peak. I particularly recall the time when Ashok Varshneya and Ashok Berry, both very well-known and highly-regarded pracharaks (especially Berry), had been summoned to Rajasthan for questioning. Jaitley, of course, was never officially the lawyer for any of them, but his legal counsel stood them in good stead. It was, in fact, from Jaitley, for the first time, that I got an idea of the whole conspiracy. His meticulous analysis gave me a fair idea that the entire set of cases billed as 'Hindu terror' were probably not what they were made out to be. Let me add here that I am referring to the period when the entire establishment was speaking in one voice, and Hindu terror or Saffron terror was being unfolded in the media like a daily soap opera. Though there were some people raising questions on the back-to-back stories, most were not quite sure what was happening, and understandably so.

A Swayamsevak Remembers

One can have questions and counter questions about what the RSS top brass say about any subject. One might even say these senior functionaries are seasoned political persons and therefore they 'know' what to say. But the same can hardly be said about a common swayamsevak. This swayamsevak, who hails from a remote tribal village of Rajasthan, studied in Gujarat and works in a small office in Delhi. He explained what he had felt about the whole thing when he was a regular shakha-goer and was committed to fulfilling whatever tasks were handed out to him by the seniors. He had felt tremendously positive about being associated with the society through his shakha. Needless to say, he never envisaged rising high in the RSS ranks or nursed any political ambitions whatsoever. He, like thousands of others, was a simple swayamsevak and nothing more. But he also shared with me in some detail how the shakhas dealt with the challenge at their own level, while Hindu terror accusations were flying thick and fast all around them. In fact, my candid conversation with this simple down-to-earth swayamsevak was more revealing and insightful compared to the top functionaries I spoke to earlier. I am just putting in brief here some of the experiences that this young, tech-savvy, bright professional and swayamsevak of many years shared with me.

He recalled aloud how he was living in Gujarat those days but had come back to his native village in Rajasthan for a break. A special meeting was convened at the local shakha where residents of neighbouring villages also joined. He recounted that the focus of the seniors, who came to address the meeting, was primarily the media. According to them, a section of the media, with active support from the then government, was trying to defame the RSS by cooking up the Hindu terror theory and in the process branding Hindus as terrorists. '*Hindu kabhi aatankvaadi nahi ho sakta[11]*' was stressed in these meetings repeatedly, and the assertion would be followed by a brief on the philosophy, traditions and values enshrined in our scriptures.

Everyone in the shakha or these *bauddhik* (intellectual) sessions was exhorted to go out into society and propagate the same views to remove any seeds of doubt that may have started germinating in the minds of Hindus. To help with the exercise, enough literature was provided as well. Another important argument put forth was that none of those who had serious cases against them were actually RSS cadres. However, they were being projected as so just because they also believed in the larger concept of the '*Hindu Vichar*' (Hindu thought).

---

11 *Hindu kabhi aatankvaadi nahi ho sakta*: A Hindu cannot be a terrorist

'Armed with all these arguments, we first went around the village and *mohallas*[12] and subsequently held gatherings of young people in colleges and local community centres,' the young man explained. We were all working under the guidance of the *Prachar Vibhag*, and our activities were being carefully planned by the topmost functionaries. Prachar Vibhag is that wing or department of the RSS which is responsible for the dissemination of the ideology, particularly among the middle classes and intellectually 'aware' segment of the Hindu society. In that sense, the Prachar Vibhag can loosely be termed the media wing of the Sangh.

From this swayamsevak's candid explanation, it is clear that though the RSS top brass claimed not to be perturbed by the allegations officially, they had to rise to the challenge swiftly and mobilise their cadres to do what was possible under the circumstances. Of course, they did not take to the streets or anything, except a one-day peaceful dharna, but they did have to reach out to everyone from the top down to the shakha level so as to ensure that the faith in the organisation did not falter.

An Insider's Damning Revelations

The most damning revelations and perhaps also the most insider account so far of how Hindu terror was the

---

12 *mohallas*: An area of a town or village

result of a conspiracy hatched at the highest level has come from former bureaucrat and author RVS Mani. When I met this exceptionally bold officer and erudite speaker for the first time, I had several hours of non-stop conversation with him in his compact and comfortable living room. It was a particularly wrong time to turn up, though, because his flat was being painted and woodwork repaired. Wherever I turned, I saw only hardbound books and paperbacks stacked up in a hurry. Apart from the books, the only other noticeable things were pictures and idols of Hindu Gods. Since the wife was away for work, Mr Mani had to fetch water for me himself. This one act alone was enough to set him apart from almost all the other bureaucrats I have known in my life.

RVS Mani is not a man of few words. But he does not believe in speaking one word beyond the subject in hand. In that sense, he is certainly not the guy for small talk. After the briefest queries about my background, he came straight to the subject. No warm-up fundas here. Once he started, I hardly needed to ask him any questions. He seemed to know exactly what I wanted and explained things in such a sequential, logical and convincing manner that I have to admit no single conversation had ever been this fruitful for me from the writing perspective. Our usual experience, as other reporters would also concur, is to constantly prod the person, ask multiple questions, reframe-rephrase the questions a few times before one can really get the picture as desired.

Mani asked me how abreast I was with the details of the conspiracy of Hindu terror or Saffron terror in the backdrop of the politico-security set-up of the country. I told him what I had gathered from my day-to-day reporting on the subject during the period in question. I also shared my impressions on his book *The Myth of Hindu Terror* which I had read more than once from cover to cover. 'If you have read my book so keenly Mishraji, then I need not go into the background. Let me come straight to the point. And this is about how the conspiracy of Hindu terror was built. As God would have it, I learnt about it very early on.'

And with that Mani started narrating what he had discussed in his book and even shared during some 'talks' organised many years after the period of reference. He took me back to the attack on the Indian Institute of Science, Bengaluru on 28 December 2005. Within two months, on 7 March 2006, there were attacks at the Varanasi Cantt Railway Station and the historic Sankat Mochan temple. Now from March 9-15, a group of LeT terrorists got nabbed by the agencies in the Aurangabad-Malegaon belt, referred to as the Ahmedabad arms haul case in the media. In his capacity as an officer who was privy to all the intelligence inputs real time, Mani claimed the cache was, 'as per technical experts, adequate to wage a war…a low-intensity, limited war!!' Besides explosives and weapons, the recovery included state-of-the-art communication equipment and gadgets. It was also learnt that the arms haul was meant to target vital installations of the country and the RSS headquarters was also one of the targets. Eventually, there 'was' an attack on the RSS Ahmedabad headquarter on 1 June 2006. That very day, Mani was called to the Union Home Minister's office in North Block. Since all the officers above him were away from the capital, and most of them were in Islamabad for an annual conference, he presumed it was to discuss the RSS office attack.

At this stage, Mani came to narrate the incident which I had already read about, yet it sent a chill down my spine when I heard him say it first-hand. The chilling story, in fact, stunned me into silence during the one-hour ride back from his residence and kept me awake for several nights to come.

'When I entered his office, Shivraj Patil, the Home Minister, was sitting on his chair. Two people were on the sofa – Digvijay Singh and another gentleman, who I later came to know was Hemant Karkare. Shivraj Patil did not say anything. These two people kept asking me about one terror case after another. I kept giving them details of the cases. Lashkar-e-Taiba, Jamat-ud-Dawa, Harkat-ul-Jihad-al-Islami, Bangladesh, etcetera. Then they asked "*Hindu ka hoga*". I said I don't have any details, neither any inputs nor any source.'

I was all ears, my nerves were taut and my stomach was in knots. Mani continued the shocking narration…

'"There is no such information. If there is, you may find out from another division which is dealing with communal harmony," I said. They said it wasn't about communal violence. They wanted information on terror attacks by Hindu terrorists. I told them there was no such input at my desk. Thereafter, I came away and recorded the conversation for my seniors' consumption.'

Mani then explained how contradictory theories of the RSS Ahmedabad office attack started appearing in the media at a time when no such inputs had come to him as the concerned officer. In another few days, an incident of a small blast in Nanded, which had actually occurred on 20 April, was billed as the first case of Hindu terror by the authorities around mid-June. This, in itself, was highly unconventional, but even more curious was the fact that CBI investigations had already revealed that the person behind the attack had engineered the low-intensity minor explosion just to extract a false insurance claim!! However, while being a small town trader, the person involved in the blast had also had an old association with the Bajrang Dal, and that became the basis for the incident being termed as Hindu terror. For all practical purposes, what was sought to be done in that infamous North Block meeting had come to be established.

Mani also gave me a first-hand account of few other terror cases which were investigated as LeT attacks and attacks assisted by local SIMI operatives but later got billed as Hindu terror. Most important among them was the Samjhauta Blast as Mani had the occasion to rush to the blast site within a few hours and got the details straight from the officers on the spot. What happened later has already been explained above in the list of incidents labelled as Hindu terror.

The Rakesh Maria Endorsement

Many have questioned the revelations made by top cop Rakesh Maria in his book which came out in February 2020 on the grounds that he should have spoken out earlier. Well, the title of the book itself is his defence. He named his book '*Let Me Say It Now*' and for obvious reasons. As a serving police officer, he could not have authored it anyway. But almost all the 'talked about' revelations in his book (at least the ones which pertain to 26/11 – the worst terror attack on Indian soil) are part of the charge-sheet filed after the investigations. To put it in one line, he explained how there was a clear attempt to label the Mumbai attacks as 'Hindu terror' and there was a concerted well-thought-out plan behind it. And it is not just the '*kalava*' theory (Kalava is a red-maroon coloured thread tied on the wrist by Indians and denotes a ritual). Identity cards were also recovered from the terrorists bearing Hindu names as students from universities in the South. Ajmal Kasab, caught alive by the brave Mumbai Police Constable Tukaram Omble, was given the cover name Samir Dinesh Chaudhary. The only reason I am mentioning the book here is because it is another stamp on RVS Mani and some other experts' claim that Hindu terror was a bogey built up to defame the majority community of the country and in a bid to create some monkey balancing. That this would bail out the real threat of Islamic terror modules spreading like wildfire throughout Maharashtra, North Kerala, Karnataka, Madhya Pradesh and Uttar Pradesh did not bother the powers. Not to mention the impression it created of Hindus as terrorists at the global level, thus falling for the ISI's game plan lock, stock and barrel.

Abhinav Bharat

Put together all the Hindu terror cases and have a look through them. Some names are common in all the cases, while many others are specific to one or two cases. However, one name which figures from the beginning to end in each of these cases is Abhinav Bharat, a social organisation primarily based in Maharashtra and Madhya Pradesh. The common refrain in all the news briefs those days was that the organisation, which was ideologically nationalist, had been 'hijacked' by extremist elements who wanted to wage a war against Islamic terror. These 'elements' were preparing for an armed struggle, and the membership was largely taken over by a lethal combination of former defence personnel and highly-radicalised Hindu extremists.

The first time Abhinav Bharat's name flashed in concern with a terror case was following the arrest of Lt Col Prasad Shrikant Purohit for the Malegaon blast. Subsequently, the organisation was named again and again in the context of the Samjhauta Blast, Ajmer Sharif and the Mecca Masjid attacks. Some reports also named Abhinav Bharat for the Jalna Mosque attacks.

There are conflicting reports about the origin of the Abhinav Bharat outfit which was referred to in these cases. The Anti-Terrorism Squad's (ATS) investigations claimed that the organisation was founded in 2006 by a retired Army Officer Major Ramesh Upadhyaya with help from Lt Col Purohit. The latter, however, submitted in the courts, as well as in the two courts of inquiry instituted by the Indian Army, that he was never a member of any organisation including this one. But before we discuss Purohit's 'association' with Abhinav Bharat, it is imperative to understand its history and background.

The Abhinav Bharat referred to here was headed by Himani Savarkar, the wife of Veer Savarkar's nephew or more clearly his brother's daughter-in-law. Himani, who became the President, claimed that she had revived the historic Abhinav Bharat founded by Vinayak Damodar Savarkar in order to propagate his ideology.

This Abhinav Bharat must not be confused with the Abhinav Bharat Charitable Trust, run by one Pankaj

Phadnis of Mumbai. This trust was established in 2001 and registered as per rules. It enjoys all the tax exemptions and other relevant benefits under the rules. We will also come to that soon. First the glorious history of the original Abhinav Bharat.

Veer Savarkar's Abhinav Bharat

Vinayak Damodar Savarkar was hardly sixteen years of age when the Chapekar brothers were hanged to death for killing the British Officer WC Rand. The hangings agitated the young Vinayak so much that he decided to devote his life to the emancipation of his Motherland. This young revolutionary's extraordinary organising skills and his zeal led to the formation of two new organisations in the Nashik-Pune area – the Rashtrabhakta Samuha and the Mitra Mela. The Mitra Mela, a social organisation, focused on debates, discussions, social activities and festivals like the Ganesh Utsav. It also contributed towards igniting the spark of revolution in the minds of its young members. It was this Mitra Mela which later transformed into the historic Abhinav Bharat Society in 1904. Mitra Mela was founded in 1899. By then Savarkar had shifted to Pune as he was enrolled in the Fergusson College. Savarkar is credited with the formation of several other societies and organisations besides Abhinav Bharat, both in India and London. It was owing to his exceptional leadership and organising skills that Abhinav Bharat

Society kept spreading all over the country, far beyond Maharashtra, with units in almost every town even after its founder had shifted to London. And we are talking of early twentieth century when means of communication were extremely limited. There are enough anecdotal and documentary evidences to suggest that Savarkar had put together such a dedicated and energetic team of associates that Abhinav Bharat's activities kept expanding both geographically and qualitatively, and the founder just had to pass on instructions or provide the proverbial 'moral support' to them from time to time. Legends of the period such as Acharya Kripalani, Madam Cama, Sikandar Hayat Khan, Balasaheb Kher, Harnam Singh and others were active members of the organisation. In 1952, Savarkar decided to dissolve the entire Abhinav Bharat structure which he had built up as a young man with his own hands. His argument was that India having attained independence, there was no need for any organisation that called for an armed struggle. While announcing the dissolution, he called upon the youth to join the Indian armed forces, instead, to strengthen and serve the nation.

Abhinav Bharat Charitable Trust

Coming back to the early 2000s, a cursory enquiry reveals that there are at least eight social outfits in far corners of the country operating under the name Abhinav Bharat.

However, for purposes of this book, we are limiting our discussion to just a couple of them.

When the alleged role of Abhinav Bharat was the toast of the media and political circles all over, one Pankaj Phadnis filed a Public Interest Litigation (PIL) in the Bombay High Court claiming that their organisation, called the Abhinav Bharat Charitable Trust, was the 'real' Abhinav Bharat, and hence the outfit headed by Himani Savarkar was an impostor and must be declared as such. Phadnis, who introduced himself as the Settlor and Advisory Trustee, complained that their trust was getting a bad name, and that they were compelled to give explanations to the world owing to the activities of Himani's outfit.

Soon after filing the PIL, Pankaj Phadnis, an engineer by profession, had issued a press release in which he said he had demanded that the Abhinav Bharat named by the Anti-Terrorism Squad ought to be named Maha-Abhinav Bharat or some such name in order to distinguish it from his trust. He even expressed shock while conversing with media persons and questioned the other organisation's claim to Veer Savarkar's legacy. In a report by *indiatoday.in* published on 17 November 2008, Phadnis was quoted as questioning, 'How can they propagate an ideology of hate based on Veer Savarkar's organisation?'. He also reiterated his claim to the freedom fighter's ideology on the grounds of 'inclusive thought' and 'unity'.

The Radical Abhinav Bharat

I now come to that Abhinav Bharat which has been at the centre of the entire Hindu terror debate. As noted above, Himani Savarkar, who is Veer Savarkar's nephew's wife, revived or re-launched the Abhinav Bharat Society in mid-2006 along with a handful of associates. Besides being married into the Savarkar family, Himani is also a relative of Nathuram Godse. A historian by profession, she is said to have concentrated on issues of social relevance. She held awareness programmes on burning problems such as terrorism. Here begins the tricky part. Lots of stories were published while the investigations were on about how Himani Savarkar's supposed social organisation had been taken over by radical Hindutva extremists gunning for an armed resistance against Islamic terrorists to 'give them back in their own coin.'

I would like to quote one such story here by Chandan Haygunde published in the *Indian Express* on 2 November 2008. The story explained, on the basis of official sources in the ATS, how the investigators felt Himani Savarkar was a genuine activist, but her organisation had been hijacked by 'army officers', along with some hardliners in the outfit, who 'motivated young Hindu men to take up arms for combating terrorism'. In a subsequent paragraph, Haygunde wrote, '…hardliners in the organisation, having an army background, who believed in Savarkar's armed struggle concept, took control as they felt the government was not firm in handling Islamic terror.'

As is clear from the date of the news copy, it was published just at the time when Lt Col Purohit was picked up by the ATS and being shifted from one jail to another for 'questioning'. This story serves as a window to most of the news stories which were being published those days.

CHARGES FALL APART GRADUALLY

Plot to Kill RSS Chief

While cases against individuals have a chequered history, the various charges levelled against Abhinav Bharat as an institution started falling apart even as early as 2010-2011. One of these cases was about the plot to kill RSS chief Mohan Madhukarrao Bhagwat. Abhinav Bharat functionaries reacted very sharply against the allegation saying that they had the utmost respect for the RSS and its chief as they were ideologically aligned in many ways, and that this was a political ploy of the Nationalist Congress Party (NCP) to drive a wedge for narrow political interests.

MHA Turns Down Demand for Ban

The Congress-NCP alliance Maharashtra government had sent a plea to the then Union Home Ministry for a ban on Abhinav Bharat under the Unlawful Activities Prevention Act (UAPA) for its 'continuing terror activities'. In a story published in the *Times of India* dated 22 August 2013, ace reporter Bharti Jain wrote, 'The Union Home Ministry has turned down Maharashtra government's plea to ban Abhinav Bharat, the radical Hindutva outfit named in several cases of saffron terror, on grounds of insufficient evidence of its continuing "terror activities" over the last two to three years.' Elaborating on the move, Jain quoted some official sources who said that the material in hand wasn't substantial enough to establish that Abhinav Bharat was involved in 'terror activities'. 'To ensure that a ban under UAPA stands the court's scrutiny and is also upheld by a review committee mandatory under the act, we have to have exhaustive material documenting the terror activities of the outfit sought to be banned, its funding, leadership and cadre still on the loose and the threat it would pose in the absence of a ban,' the home ministry official is quoted as having said.

Nor were there enough inputs about the structure of the organisation, its cadre and its leadership who may be plotting or running terror modules. Security agencies also did not find any links or tracks for funding of such activities, said the story quoting MHA sources.

Individual Ban Vs Organisational Ban

As any security expert will confirm, it is much easier to contemplate and impose a ban on individual entities for any unlawful activity or threat. In case of an individual, his or her involvement in any such activity even once is enough not only to take action (as is wont) but also put the person under constant watch and even sundry restrictions. However, the case of banning an organisation is a much more complicated and exhaustive process. The government or the agency proposing to ban any outfit must provide sufficient evidence, over a sufficiently satisfactory period of time, of the organisation having indulged in the unlawful activity 'as an organisation'. In other words, this means that the leadership and the machinery of the organisation must be involved at an 'institutional' level with the said unlawful acts. Involvement of certain individuals who have committed an unlawful act is 'not' enough to impose a ban. Needless to say it is more challenging to impose a ban on an organisation rather than individuals.

Who Actually Revived Abhinav Bharat?

This question may appear strange and even unnecessary to most people. The common impression is that Himani Savarkar, along with a handful of like-minded persons, revived or re-launched the Abhinav Bharat outfit. However, an officer who served in the Ministry of Home Affairs and was involved in the audit work (apart from other responsibilities) during the UPA I and part of UPA II shared some information which shook me enough to pursue him for several weeks and possibly dig deep into what outwardly appeared to be, in our reporter's language, a very 'antiseptic' kind of information. For obvious reasons, it is not prudent to divulge the name of the officer here, but what he told me could throw a new light on the entire Hindu terror theory. It would also lend credence to the apprehension put forth by some experts that the Hindu terror conspiracy or the sinister plan to devise an equivalence against Islamic terror which was spreading its tentacles in every corner of India was not a sudden development but being 'worked upon' over a fairly longer period.

I came across a highly placed official source, along with another journalist friend, in a chance meeting somewhere in South Delhi. After following up our acquaintance on phone a few times, I had a longish sitting one afternoon. As we got talking, he started telling me how funds meant for security-related purposes were often diverted into all kinds of weird projects.

Now this was something I did not need to be explained. My reporting career started in Jammu and Kashmir and I cut my teeth scanning the villages located on the International Border and the Line of Control. Those were the days when terrorism was at its peak. Blasts in public places like railway platforms and cinema theatres were common headlines in cities like Jammu, and massacres in the remote areas kept us on our toes. Even heavy mortar shelling along the border was not considered worthy of page one. And to say that the working of the government in the turmoil-ridden state was 'different' would be an understatement. There were dozens of issues which the celebrity journalists swooping on the state after a big terror attack would never understand. One of these was the curious case of Security-Related-Expenditure which everybody in the administration and the media referred to as SRE. For some strange reason, the full term was never pronounced. So the unwritten rule was 'anything' which had to bypass scrutiny had to be routed somehow through the SRE. Once that was done, it would be above questions. In those days, it was the Farooq Abdullah-led government. But this also applied to other governments preceding and succeeding him.

Now this MHA officer shared with me how, while working closely with the Home Minister's office, he had 'chanced upon' some funds being pumped to support some social organisation in the same area where Abhinav Bharat is said to have been active initially. This involves accounts which can probably never come out in the public domain, nor could there have been much documentation to investigate except perhaps some bank transactions at the topmost level. Hence I will have to leave it at that.

But before dismissing me from meeting him again in future, this officer did give me another hint even as things appeared more muddled than ever. In a counter-questioning tone, he said, if there was such a clincher of evidence against the Abhinav Bharat organisation in almost every case of alleged Hindu terror, and it had become the hub of terror activities, why did the centre refrain from banning the organisation? What held them back from taking any further steps at a time when things were so hot? And it may be noted that the decision to not ban Abhinav Bharat was not based on any technical grounds as it happens sometimes in such cases. The Centre, Ministry of Home Affairs to be precise, categorically rejected the Maharashtra government's proposal. Why and how it was done has already been elaborated in the above paragraphs. But the question that still haunts me is: why did the MHA take a completely contrary view to the one proposed by the ATS, particularly when they were pushing the Hindu terror theory so aggressively in their political statements all this while? Certainly, something did not add up here.

But one small yet crucial point needs to be flagged here before I wind up the subject which has evoked sharp and passionate reactions from people on both sides of the political spectrum. When exactly did Abhinav Bharat make its appearance in its new avatar? Nobody seems to know for sure. A Home Ministry report of 2013 says this happened in 2006, and Abhinav Bharat, which was reportedly set up to counter Jihadi terrorism, was mainly operating in Maharashtra and Madhya Pradesh. Now the question is whether this Abhinav Bharat was started as a new chapter of the same old Veer Savarkar's historic organisation, or was it a completely new outfit? If it started as a renewed avatar of the old organisation, how was this applied for since Veer Savarkar had ordered the dissolution of the organisation throughout the country!

So, let us assume that it was registered as a completely new outfit. Then there must have been an application to this effect somewhere in Maharashtra or even Madhya Pradesh. But there seems to be no record of such a registration or even an application in any of these states. The only record available is the launching of a website in the name of Abhinav Bharat. The registration of the website is dated 19 May 2007 in Nashik, Maharashtra.

To cut a long story short, the revival of the Abhinav Bharat, touted as the launch pad of all Hindu terror cases, remains shrouded in mystery lending more credence to the theory of my source. To repeat what I said above, something just did not add up.

Abhinav Bharat and Lt Col Shrikant Purohit

The strongest 'evidence' presented against Lt Col Purohit, so far as his association with Abhinav Bharat is concerned, was the report of a meeting held in Faridabad on 25/26 January 2008. It is claimed that Purohit, along with a group of associates, had planned a series of blasts with the help of some Hindu radicals to avenge terror attacks by Jihadi forces. Without going too much into details, which have already been published umpteen times and have been floating in the public domain for years, I will come to specific statements made in this context to help understand what might have happened.

One of the most crucial prosecution witnesses Lt Col Bappaditya Dhar's testimony can give a fairly good idea of things. While giving his statement, Lt Col Dhar is quoted as having said that right after the meeting, in which the challenge of Islamic/Jihadi terror spreading its tentacles in many sensitive regions of the country was discussed at length, he found Lt Col Purohit in the corridor speaking to some people on the phone. It may be noted that Dhar was also present throughout the meeting. In the meeting, Purohit had reportedly stressed on the importance of having an organisation which can work towards fighting this challenge. When he asked Purohit privately what the meeting was about and the overall plan, the latter told him it was part of a larger covert operation he was working on. Purohit then asked to be excused so that he could make a few phone calls and update his senior officers about the developments. Lt Col Dhar then related how he overheard Purohit briefing two officers back-to-back on the phone. While talking on the first phone call, Purohit said he had informed Col Raikar, and on the second call he said he had informed Col Panchpore about 'everything'.

It is relevant to mention here that Col SS Raikar was a senior officer in the chain of command while Col VS Panchpore was the Commanding Officer of the unit in Deolali which Purohit was serving before he was picked up by the ATS. Hence, the significance of the witness statement mentioned above cannot be discounted by anyone. An officer, hatching a 'conspiracy' of such serious proportions as a terror attack on innocent citizens, is hardly expected to rush out to the corridor and promptly report to his unit bosses about the developments of the day and keep them updated at regular intervals. He would rather have done his best to keep things under wraps and try not to discuss things with another army officer from a different part of the country.

Lt Col Bappaditya Dhar's testimony doesn't end here. He appears once again in the context of another meeting held in Kolkata. Here too his statement unambiguously underlines that Lt Col Purohit's efforts to gain access to the Maoist network in Nepal had nothing to do with any 'personal' agenda or conspiracy. Whatever Purohit may have had in mind, not only were his seniors well aware of these meetings, but he was keeping them promptly updated of every development.

Though Lt Col Bappaditya Dhar's statements are quite sufficient in themselves, I cannot miss out a couple of more witnesses on the all-important issue of Purohit's association with the Abhinav Bharat. Let us check out another interesting witness here. Dr RP Singh was working for the Intelligence Bureau in areas of Uttar Pradesh bordering Nepal. This is a telephone conversation quoted in the case file where Purohit asks Dr RP Singh whether the cell numbers he had given were right or not. Singh replies they were all correct and he is 'on the job' but it is not enough because they need sources within the Maoist network of Nepal. Purohit then directed Dr RP Singh to the top officers at the Intelligence and Field Security Unit (IFSU), a military unit stationed at Gorakhpur, monitoring the activities of the Maoists in and from Nepal. I have a larger chunk of the conversation between Lt Col Purohit and Dr RP Singh in my notes but I am not putting them here as they involve relations between two friendly neighbours with robust diplomatic ties.

But I would certainly like to quote a statement of Col SS Raikar who, as mentioned above, was a senior officer in Purohit's unit at Deolali. During witness examination, Col Raikar had clearly stated that he remembered how Purohit called him right after his meetings in Faridabad and shared some serious inputs about the activities of Maoists in Nepal posing threat to the security of our country. To help him further on this, Raikar recalled how he had provided the contact numbers of Col Roy, Commanding Officer of IFSU, Gorakhpur and Col Bhattacharya, Commanding Officer of IFSU, Kolkata. These were the same officers whose numbers Purohit had shared with RP Singh to help him cultivate sources in the Maoist ranks and monitor their plans. Lt Col Bappaditya Dhar, whose all-important statement has already been quoted above briefly, also mentions how Purohit had held meetings in Kolkata where they discussed ideas to cultivate a network of Bangladeshi youth, details of which I consider too sensitive to be shared here. Even Col Raikar had confirmed about the plan in his statement.

Just to add one more name here, a witness Tapan Ghosh also testified that he was present in one of the meetings. According to Ghosh, there did not appear any hint of a conspiracy, leave alone any terrorist angle during the discussions. However, he remarked that Lt Col Purohit did propose the formation of a political outfit. Ghosh wasn't sure whether it was part of an official plan or Purohit's individual initiative. In any case, he said nobody was enthused by the proposal.

The idea of bringing in these witness statements of senior Army and intelligence officers here is simple. That the meetings, visits and contacts of Lt Col Purohit, which were projected by the prosecution as part of his terror plans, were actually his field visits and meetings undertaken as part of his intelligence gathering and related exercises.

Two parallel, antithetical views on Lt Col Purohit's association with the controversial Abhinav Bharat have been before us. One, that Purohit was an Army officer with delusions of Hindutva supremacy and hatred for Islamic/Jihadi violence. The hatred consumed him so much that he decided to misuse his position as a Military Intelligence officer to gather a handful of like-minded radical Hindu elements, organised them, provided them arms through his defence contacts and then engineered blasts at various places in the country to 'avenge' terror attacks by Islamic terrorists. And all this was done through the platform of Abhinav Bharat, an organisation formed to create awareness for national issues and instil patriotism, which was hijacked by radicals like Purohit and some of his associates both inside and outside the armed forces. This view was propounded by the ATS and therefore finds mention in all media reports. As underlined in a previous chapter, this view was widely shared in the global media too and particularly in Pakistan.

The other view is held and shared by people who claim they actually 'know' what happened. These are the people who are old friends, colleagues, associates and contacts of Purohit. There are some others who do not belong to any of these categories and never knew or met Purohit personally but claim they know the facts by dint of their official position. This view is that Purohit was hot on the trail of extremist Islamic organisations like SIMI and had managed to infiltrate quite deep into their network. In his pursuit of information, he could not possibly do a lot of things by himself as his activities had alerted the elements already. It had become very difficult for him to expose himself beyond a point. Hence he, along with a couple of like-minded colleagues, decided to utilise the network of the Abhinav Bharat in penetrating into the enemy's ranks to gather valuable information through covert operations. The reason they chose this organisation was it already had manpower which was passionately patriotic, ready to risk themselves and also familiar with the necessary know-how. 'I couldn't possibly have come out in the open and exposed myself or my colleagues. Like me, few people in the Abhinav Bharat were seriously concerned about the way SIMI and other terrorist networks were spreading into each district and they were ready to help me through their local contacts and knowledge,' Purohit is learnt to have told one of these associates soon after he came out of jail. 'When you are in hot pursuit of the enemies of the nation, every step you take cannot be black or white. There are shades of grey involved keeping the end goal in mind,' he is said to have argued. It was these shades of grey, his friends claim, which came in handy for the ATS and the powers-that-be in implicating the officer.

One Arrest, Many Questions

It is natural for a common Indian to get sceptical about the truth of the conspiracy of Hindu terror. Even if one weren't sceptical, one can be easily confused by the contradictory arguments and information in the public domain. For all such people, the best way to wade through the muddle would be to know how and in what manner Lt Col Prasad Shrikant Purohit was taken captive exactly a month after the Malegaon blast of September 2008. A look into the events could actually open many people's eyes. Both the manner and the sequence of the arrest was so bizarre that several army officers I spoke to and who are privy to the developments said they were baffled by the situation and the inherent contradictions of the 'arrest'.

To understand what happened and how, I am relating here the turn of events from the time Purohit was 'picked up' in Pachmarhi, Madhya Pradesh, till the time he was handed over to the Anti-Terror Squad (hereby referred to as ATS) Mumbai. This was exactly a one-week period, as he was taken captive on 29 October 2008 but formally shown as arrested by the ATS only on 6 November 2008.

Purohit Taken Captive in Madhya Pradesh

On 29 September 2008, a bomb exploded at the Bhikku Chowk in the textile town of Malegaon late in the evening. Details of the blast have already been given in a previous chapter. Exactly a month later, Purohit was picked up from a training facility in Pachmarhi where he was pursuing a course in Arabic language. On 29 October, he was brought by road to Bhopal and informed that he had been ordered to move to New Delhi for a new assignment. The whole operation was led by Col RK Srivastava (or RKS) about whom we shall know more, later in this chapter. Through the entire road trip, Lt Col Purohit kept asking RKS the reason for these sudden orders and what was the tearing hurry to make him cut short his training. But he did not get any answers. Just that these were the standing orders and had to be implemented without any further delay. Col Purohit, as per his own statement, was given a Movement Order for Delhi. But it was at the Raja Bhoj Airport in Bhopal, where they drove to straight from Pachmarhi, that Purohit realised he was not to travel to New Delhi at all. He was, in fact, made to board a flight to Mumbai instead. This change in destination was told to him at the time of getting the boarding pass, and he was neither given nor shown any Movement Order for Mumbai. Both these facts have been corroborated by at least two senior officers, a Lt Col rank officer and a Brigadier. Both of them appeared as witnesses in the Army Court of Inquiry, testified and corroborated it. Lt Col GC Mohanta and Brigadier Raj Kumar are the two senior officers referred to here.

After reaching Mumbai, till he was shown as being 'formally arrested' by the ATS, Purohit was kept captive. Under what rule this was done is anybody's guess. Obviously, it was an illegal detention to put it in simple language. But that also was not without its drama and contradictions and many, many unexplained and sinister questions.

To understand how 'unusual' it all was and baffling at so many levels, let us once look at the developments in descending order or in a 'backward' sequence. Lt Col Purohit was handed over to the ATS on 5 November 2008. This handing over was done by the officiating CO, Provost Unit, MG & G Area on the orders of Maj Gen Hooda, GOC of the same area. In the Indian Army, the MG & G Area stands for Maharashtra, Gujarat and Goa. The order was dated 4 November where Purohit is referred to as an officer of the Provost Unit, MG & G Area. But Purohit is on record on various occasions that the entire paperwork was suspect because he was never taken on strength or parade in this unit at any point of time, either on reaching Mumbai or even after the arrest. The same was corroborated by Lt Col S Verma in the Army's internal Inquiry. Verma testified that neither was the subject taken on strength or in parade state of Provost Unit anytime between 29 October and 5 November.

In Army parlance, a person joining a particular unit needs to be taken on parade or to be precise 'parade state'. This procedure is known as 'taken on strength'. In layman terms, unless and until a person has been taken on strength, he or she is not considered to be a part of the unit. This, in turn, also means he or she cannot be ordered or employed or even sent off to any other unit by the unit in reference.

Now here is another set of testimonies even more baffling than the earlier. Lt Col (Retd) Jitender Sharma who was then the officiating CO of the Provost Unit was also the officer who 'formally' handed over Purohit to the ATS. Col Sanjay Nand and Col GS Mohanta (mentioned above) were also there in the headquarter, MG & G area. These three officers are on record that Lt Col Purohit was brought to the station only on November 4, that too late evening. Which means he spent barely one night there before his formal arrest.

Now the pertinent questions:

- Where and with whom was Purohit between 29 October and the evening of 4 November? What was his location?
- Was he on a Movement Order or in custody?
- If he was in captivity, who had ordered that captivity?
- He was shown as having been handed over by the Provost Unit. But at least three officers testified during the Court of Inquiry that he was neither taken on strength nor on parade by the said unit, either before or after the arrest, then how and why was he being termed as an officer of that unit?
- If there was indeed a Movement Order to the Provost Unit for Purohit, there certainly would have been several questions from the CO and other senior officers over his non-reporting to the Unit. There would certainly have been enquiries as to why the process was not completed. This brings us to the moot question which is bound to nag everyone who tries to put the entire sequence in perspective – What exactly was the Movement Order for Lt Col Purohit? Was there any order at all? If yes, what unit or place was it actually for? If his orders were indeed for the Provost Unit MG & G Area, why wasn't he made to report there right after landing in Mumbai?

Before we try to get to the bottom of the entire maze of unexplained events, a primer on these 'Movement Orders'. Whenever a serving Army personnel goes out for 'Temporary Duty' he is issued a Movement Order, invariably signed by the Adjutant of the unit or establishment. A copy is retained for record while another copy sent by post to the unit where the officer must report. The officer is then handed his Movement Order. Once issued, no one other than the issuing authority or the destination unit can make an amendment to the Movement Order.

Why these boring obvious kind of bureaucratic formalities related to movements and routine functions become so relevant in the context of Purohit's arrest will be clear in just a few subsequent paragraphs. Because it is in the alleged forgery, or, may I say, alleged 'tampering' of the Movement Order that the answers to a lot of our questions lie buried. But hold on....

What Was Col RK Srivastava up to?
Did RKS Weave a Web of Lies, Forgery?

To find the answers to each of these questions, one has perforce to look at the role of Col RK Srivastava since Purohit was completely at the mercy of this one officer right from Pachmarhi till he was taken into custody by the ATS. The former was calling all the shots and controlling or manipulating all that was happening. Actually RKS' role extended far beyond the arrest, but we shall come to that later.

First things first. It had become clear at the Bhopal airport itself that Purohit would not be travelling to Delhi but to Mumbai instead. So the order about Delhi was obviously a lie. But there was an 'Order'. So what did it say? My research of the case shows the original order was for 3 DET Southern Command, Liaison Unit, Colaba Mumbai. So, as per procedure, Purohit should have reported straight at this Unit on landing in Mumbai. However, things happened too swiftly from here. His phone was snatched away from him. He had no access to any means of communication by which he could check what was going on. As it is, not showing the incumbent officer his movement orders by itself is illegal or at least highly inappropriate. On top of that, the Movement Order was meant for Military Intelligence – 20 (MI-20) and should have gone by post to the concerned unit from the AEC Centre. In other words, the letter order should not even have been in the possession of Col Srivastava in the first place. On reaching Mumbai, Srivastava was joined by an IB officer Sanjay Garg. Both of them put Purohit in a Tata Sumo vehicle and drove to an unidentified location somewhere in Khandala where he was housed in a bungalow. What sort of things were tried on him during the illegal captivity will be discussed in subsequent pages of this book. But indications of these physical and mental tortures have appeared in some sections of the media from time to time – the beatings, physical trauma, the insults and abuses in a bid to force him to confess to acts of terror and abetment to terror almost on the lines of a scripted plan.

With no orders in hand, no phone and no means to find out where he was holed up, Purohit was practically in illegal captivity ever since he left Pachmarhi. People, including his wife and family, came to know only much later that during this one-week period, the decorated senior Army Officer was confined to a house in Khandala with zero access to either any official or personal contact.

With responsible officers in the concerned unit having testified on record that Purohit wasn't taken on strength or parade by the unit, the only mystery that remains to be unravelled is: if the original Movement Order was for 3 DET, how did the Provost Unit come into the picture at all? Lt Col Purohit, in his statements in the court of law and much more specifically in the army's enquiry, had stated that this was nothing but a case of forging or falsification of documents. To the best of my knowledge, the prosecution had been unable to explain the mystery of the destination and the temporary matter in the court of law.

I have already explained how Movement Orders are sent to all concerned authorities, besides, of course, being handed to the incumbent. Now, when the document reaches any officer's desk, it is imprinted with the First Dak Stamp along with the initials of the Officer on whose desk the communication lands.

Now this is where the sinister game plan by RKS seems to have unfolded. When RKS came to Pachmarhi, he is reported to have carried an ink-signed Movement Order copy meant for the DGMT MI-20. This naturally raises doubts as to where and how he wanted to take Purohit. This allowed him to take Purohit to a station for a short period during which he could plan his next move and carry out the necessary amendments.

In his statements during the Court of Inquiry, Purohit categorically charged Col Srivastava of forging the Movement Order, cutting and then changing the name of the destination unit into his own Provost Unit, MG & G Area. Later, when he produced the same, instructions were passed just before the arrest (in the nick of time) showing Purohit as an officer of that Unit.

Is there a way to check if there was indeed tampering with the original Movement Order and that RKS may have utilised the time period before the formal arrest to carry out the forgery? Well, the documents related to the move most certainly point in that direction. First, I must add that the Provost Unit was definitely not aware of Purohit joining them until just before the arrest. Had they been informed, the concerned appointments (authorities for the layman) would have enquired about the non-reporting of the incumbent for a whole week. Now for the order. The Movement Order, as submitted as evidence during investigation, did show the First Sight Dak stamp imprinted on it. But it is clouded in mystery as it did not bear the initials or signatures of any of the authorities to whom it should have been circulated and made a 'record'. But we need not play on conjecture. There is more solid and irrefutable evidence.

I turn once again to the testimony of Lt Col S Verma. Verma said on record that the First Sight Dak stamp as imprinted on the order 'did not' belong to their Provost Unit nor to the HQ, MG & G Area. He also added during his statements that there had been 'no entry' into the Dak Register of the Provost Unit at all. Anybody familiar with the functioning of the armed forces knows that any personnel, let alone a responsible officer, cannot be moved from one place to another, kept at an unknown location for almost a week, and then produced in a Unit suddenly without the necessary procedures completed. In other words, the Movement Order to Provost Unit was drafted by someone who showed an entry in the Dak stamp (interestingly not of the Provost Unit) but did not deliver the Order to the concerned authorities or appointments.

To put the whole picture in a nutshell:

- On 29 October 2008, Lt Col Purohit was picked up from the Army's training facility in Pachmarhi on the grounds of a Movement Order to New Delhi though he was only mid-way into his Arabic language training at the time. He was never shown the order by Col RK Srivastava who had come to pick him up personally.

- His mobile phone was taken away from him on the way to Bhopal thus making Purohit suspicious, worried and incommunicado.

- At Bhopal airport, it dawned on him that they were travelling to Mumbai and not Delhi. Still no order was given or shown.

- On landing in Mumbai, RKS was joined by IB Officer Sanjay Garg, and instead of reporting at the Military Intelligence Unit in Colaba (as told), he was driven in a private vehicle to an empty bungalow at an undisclosed location in Khandala.

- On 4 November 2008, he was taken back to Mumbai late in the evening. The next morning, on 5 November 2008, he was handed over to the Mumbai ATS.

- The ink-stamped letter meant for 3 DET, Southern Command Liaison Unit, Colaba, Mumbai had mysteriously changed to Provost Unit, MG & G Area. At the time of the arrest, he was named as an officer of the latter Unit though he had never been taken on strength or parade state by the said unit at all as verified by the officers themselves.

- The letter had no First Dak Stamp of the Provost Unit (as clear by the witness statements) but interestingly bore the stamp of the FSD Unit of the 'G' branch of the HQ, MG & G Area. Which brings us to another related question and/or suspicion: Did RKS forge the Movement Order and replace the destination unit as the Provost Unit and then get the First Dak stamped by the G Branch of the HQ? Is it possible that he was hopeful or even certain of having his way there by dint of his influence and because some personnel in this unit would have less or no objections to this entirely questionable and even illegal operation?

So Why Did Col RK Srivastava Do It?

People who know both RKS and Purohit as officers and/or individuals, both in the services and in the establishment in Delhi and Mumbai, say that this does not even merit a question. The answer is so obvious. But that cannot apply to common people who know neither of them, either in person or by reputation, and their impression of the entire issue is limited to stories which appeared in the media. A few select news copies or analyses, published some years after the arrest, did focus a paragraph or two on the conduct of Col Srivastava, but the only reason they could hint at was professional rivalry between the two officers. Since both were considered bright and ambitious officers of the Military Intelligence and RKS's desire to get even with Purohit (who was scoring every day in penetrating into the enemy's camp and reporting on their game plan) may have got the better of him. But the desire to score over your colleague, to outshine someone in the profession, is so common in the intelligence game that one would hardly take note of it.

I made repeated trips to Mumbai, tracking and conversing with several people who could have any or some idea of things before and after the arrest and also knew both the officers personally. Finally, I was able to form some understanding of the scenario. Why was Col RK Srivastava willing to go ahead with whatever the Anti-Terrorism Squad and, as it emerged subsequently, the political establishment wanted to be done? What's even more baffling is that RKS was not only pro-active to the extent of resorting to illegalities, he was, in fact, the one who inflicted physical tortures on Purohit during his captivity in Khandala. It must be brought out in the public domain that while ATS functionaries were present and did their best to pressurise their hostage through various means, the physical tortures inflicted by them pales before the brutality that was reportedly shown by RKS. The continuous beatings, tortures, vile abuses...all came from Srivastava. I do not intend to repeat those filthy abuses here, but it should be known to all that he did not just threaten Purohit with a lifetime in jail but also 'promised' him that his entire family, the wife, mother, sons would all be compelled to live a pauper's life, ostracised and shunned by society. He also threatened abduction, rape and murder...the kind of treatment one cannot associate even with hardened criminals, leave alone a decorated, dynamic officer and colleague.

Without going back too far into the past, I may just say here that Col RK Srivastava's constant run-ins with most colleagues and junior officers, complaints filed against him by other personnel and his 'issues' with the intelligence reports being submitted by Purohit at a surprising pace must all have been noticed by the ATS and the bigwigs in the Mumbai *sarkar* (government). This was no random move. The strategy to rope in RKS for 'picking up' Lt Col Purohit was meticulously planned; right people with the required degree of motivation were chosen to execute it. The choice of RKS could be termed 'perfect' as he was not only motivated enough to do whatever was expected of him but also ready to resort to all kinds of illegal tactics for the same. It was almost as if he was playing a game of hunting. Only the victim here was no animal in the forest but an army officer with one of the brightest careers among his peers and a man with a family and reputation.

Of course, a complaint was filed against RKS by Purohit for his conduct, and the army did conduct the inquiry but by then enough damage had been done. One of the brightest officers of his generation was languishing in jail, labelled in India and the world at large as the face of 'Hindu terror', his wife and sons running from pillar to post for justice, swallowing the tag of a terrorist's family, day in and day out.

The RDX Plant

Whether one looks at media reports of 2008-09 or the case files of the ATS, the one solid piece of evidence claimed by the prosecution on which their entire case rested was that Lt Col Prasad Shrikant Purohit used his position as a senior Army officer to provide all the logistic support, including explosives, needed for the Malegaon blast. As evidence, they produced a cache of RDX reportedly hidden in a room of one Sudhakar Chaturvedi's house. Before I go into the details of that 'recovery', it is pertinent to underline the fact that the Malegaon blast took place on 29 September 2008. Purohit was picked up on 29 October 2008, whereas this recovery came as late as 25 November 2008. Now the argument of the prosecution here was that this recovery established the fact that explosives were being arranged for more such attacks by Abhinav Bharat with help from Purohit. Just to put things in perspective, by the time this recovery was made, Purohit had already been in undeclared captivity for one week and another twenty days in jail.

After having researched on whatever is relevant to the episode, I do now want to share as much in detail as possible how this recovery was done, though it may not be a ball-by-ball account. The reason, again, being that this was presented as the most 'incriminating' evidence against the accused. The sequence of events and the subsequent statements of some of the senior army officers, who appeared as witnesses in the Army's Court of Inquiry, will give a fair idea of what must have happened.

The prosecution (ATS in this case) had claimed all through that they had conducted a house search of Sudhakar Chaturvedi's residence at Deolali Camp. Chaturvedi, referred to as Accused no 11 in the case files of the ATS, was not present there, and it was claimed in the *Panchnama*[13] that the front door of the house had to be broken open as the keys were not available with anyone. It was claimed that after a thorough search, swab samples were collected and sent for analysis at the Forensic Laboratory at Kalina, Mumbai. The sample analysis confirmed traces of RDX, the prosecution noted.

This claim or theory was widely reported, published extensively in India and abroad. However, when the Army conducted its Court of Inquiry, startling revelations were made by some crucial witnesses. These revelations did come out in the public domain, though much later, but their significance has still not been sufficiently underlined, either by the media or in the political circles. The most eye-opening witness was Subedar Keshav Karbhari Pawar, whose statement indicated in unambiguous terms that the 'evidence' of the RDX swab samples was clearly a plant. It appears very clearly from his statement that

---

13 *panchnama*: A record of witness testimony, usually prepared by the police, during the investigation of a crime or after a death.

the 'plant' could have been done by none other than the ATS itself.

As per Subedar KK Pawar's statement...

He got a call on his mobile on 3 November 2008 between 1430 to 1500 hours by one ASI Bagde of Nashik ATS asking directions to Sudhakar Chaturvedi's house. Pawar, following his discipline, immediately informed his Officer Commanding Major Praveen Khanzode who in turn flagged it with the HQ Southern Command, Liaison Unit, Pune. Very soon Pawar was asked by Major Khanzode to assist the ASI in whatever he wanted. But when Pawar called back ASI Bagde, he said he did not need the address anymore as he had been called back by his seniors and that he was already on his way back. Puzzled, Pawar promptly updated Major Khanzode of this sudden turn. But Khanzode immediately sensed something fishy here and asked Subedar Pawar to come along with him. Apart from ASI Bagde's unusual behaviour, Khanzode was also concerned because the developments had generated a lot of media attention, and he wanted to make sure there were no reporters prowling around the Army Camp.

I now shift to the statement of Major Praveen Khanzode, another crucial witness in the entire 'RDX' theory. His account more than sufficiently proves what must have happened at Sudhakar Chaturvedi's house that fateful afternoon. Here goes...

Let me pick up Major Khanzode's statement from the point where I left it above in Subedar Pawar's narration. So Khanzode recalled at the inquiry how, around 1500 hours on 3 November, Subedar Pawar called him to say that one ASI Bagde was asking for directions to Sudhakar Chaturvedi's house. Khanzode asked Pawar to wait while the former got it cleared from his own Commanding officer, Col VS Panchpore. Col Panchpore, in turn, checked it with the Brigadier General Staff Intelligence (BGS-Int) at the Southern Command HQ. In ten minutes Khanzode got the clearance from the BGS and conveyed it to Pawar, that he was to assist ASI Bagde in whatever he needed. However, he was surprised to know from Pawar that it was unnecessary now as Bagde had by then been reportedly called back by his seniors. Major Khanzode, however, was not comfortable with the turn of events. Plus, he knew that news reporters were trailing the movements of the ATS ever since the arrests of Purohit and others. Hence, just to make sure that there were no local journalists prowling around the cantonment, Khanzode asked Pawar to come along and check the area around Sudhakar Chaturvedi's house. Khanzode didn't know the house so they rode together on a Scooty. Even Pawar had some trouble locating the house as he had been there only once before. When they reached the place, Subedar Pawar went around to the backside of the quarter.

Khanzode then dropped a bombshell in his statement when he said he heard Subedar Pawar talking to someone there. When asked, Pawar said he had found the backdoor of the house open and ASI Bagde inside there. This, just few minutes after Bagde had told Pawar that he was leaving the cantonment on his seniors' orders. Bagde's behaviour was cagey and suspicious; he failed to explain why he was still there and what he was doing at Chaturvedi's house. Alarmed, Major Khanzode immediately updated the developments to his Commanding Officer Col VS Panchpore who also must have been baffled by the turn of events. Just to be doubly sure, Major Khanzode also informed the School of Artillery verbally about the curious developments and asked them to remain alert and place sentries accordingly. During the next two days, ie. on 4 ad 5 November, Khanzode said he had recounted the incident to a number of officers at the headquarters in Pune.

Looking back at the prosecution's (in this case ATS) claim that they recovered traces of RDX from the house of Sudhakar Chaturvedi on 25 November 2008 and that the nature of the explosive was confirmed in forensic testing of the swab samples, the above developments need to be put in perspective.

- That an Assistant Sub Inspector Bagde of the Nashik ATS had come looking for the same house in Deolali Camp area.

- That ASI Bagde lied to Subedar KK Pawar that he had been called back by his seniors even before reaching the house.

- That when Subedar Pawar and Major Khanzode reached the house shortly after Bagde's call, the backdoor had been opened without any signs of break-in and ASI Bagde was inside. When asked, Bagde failed to explain convincingly how he managed to get in and what he was doing there.

- That while Bagde had comfortably entered the quarter from the backdoor without breaking in, the ATS claimed they had to break open the front door when they raided the place on November 25.

- That the same quarter was named as the 'hideout' where Chaturvedi and Lt Col Purohit were accused of having hidden the RDX used for the Malegaon blasts and perhaps others too.

Clearly, a lot remained unexplained here. It has been Purohit's declared position that it was the ATS, with some 'inside assistance' from Col RK Srivastava, that 'planted' the explosives to trap him.

Most observers, including the experts on internal security I spoke to, who have been following the Hindu terror cases keenly, underlined that the witness Subedar KK Pawar's statement was sufficiently strong in establishing that the 'recovery' of RDX theory by the ATS had too many gaping holes in it. However, I would like to mention a few more witness statements here to corroborate the claim that the RDX was actually a plant against the accused and support the stunning claims made by Subedar Pawar.

Captain Nitin Dattatray Joshi and his Tale of Horrors

First the case of Captain (retired) Nitin D Joshi. This officer was touted as one of the prime witnesses by the prosecution in the context of the RDX 'recovery', the strongest pillar on which the ATS built its case. In his initial statement, Capt Joshi had corroborated the ATS's claim saying he had 'seen' a package of RDX at Purohit's house in Deolali. Coming from an Army officer, this was a major statement, and the ATS or the prosecution may have felt they got a clincher here. But a sudden twist in the 'fool-proof' statement gave a completely new dimension to the story. The same officer, Capt Nitin Dattatray Joshi, filed a serious case against the ATS with the State Human Rights Commission on 25 October 2009 where he narrated in vivid details the circumstances under which he was forced to make the damning statement. His complaint can be checked vide case no 3237/2009-10 with the State Human Rights Commission, Maharashtra.

In his petition, a mind boggling one if there was any, Capt Joshi gave complete chronology of events leading to that statement of his which became a strong weapon in the prosecution's armoury. I want to quote here excerpts from his petition to the SHRC rather than any news reports. This petition was filed in October 2009. Almost exactly a year after Purohit was picked up by the ATS. The petitioner was registered as Captain Nitin Dattatray Joshi, a resident of Thane. At that time, Joshi was serving as a Commandant at the Maharashtra Military School, Village Tokawade, Taluka Murbad. The petition described Joshi as a devoted hard-core Army officer who was deployed as Captain in 2 Sikh Light Infantry when he retired. With his qualifications, he had lucrative offers from the corporate sector, but he opted for teaching at the Bhonsala Military School in Nashik so as to motivate and develop youngsters to devote their life to the country. It was during his service at Bhonsala that he met Lt Col Prasad Purohit and was very impressed with the latter's personality, patriotism and high morals 'towards the Nation'. Purohit also introduced him to Abhinav Bharat, a social organisation, and he participated occasionally in some of its social events. This continued till Purohit was sent to Pachmarhi for his training, and subsequently Joshi learnt from news reports that he had been arrested in connection with the Malegaon blasts.

Capt Joshi's ordeal with the ATS began just a couple of days after Purohit was picked up from Pachmarhi by Col RK Srivastava. He was first called on the evening of 31 October 2008 to the ATS office in Nashik where

Shekhar Bagde (same ASI Bagde) asked him several questions about Purohit and Abhinav Bharat. Joshi replied it was atrocious that Purohit could be involved in any anti-national conspiracy. On Abhinav Bharat, he said it was a social organisation limited to social activities and events, though it was possible that they may have political intentions at a later stage. The questioning which began at 2000 hours on the evening of 31 October continued past 0200 hours on 1 November. The second call came on the evening of 7 November when Bagde said he was coming to the Bhonsala campus. Bagde, who came with three other people, repeated the same questions and got the same answers. On his way out, he told Joshi, 'You are hiding facts and we will get it from you.'

Around mid-morning on 12 November, Joshi again got a call asking him to reach the ATS office pronto even though he argued he had urgent work in the Academy and may take some time. Since Bagde wasn't ready to consider it, Joshi reached the ATS office in an hour only to be asked the same questions all over again. Plus, he was asked when and how many times had he met Sadhvi Pragya, when did he accompany Purohit to Malegaon, Kolkata, Bhopal, Jabalpur etcetera. Joshi curtly replied he had never met the Sadhvi, only read her name in the papers and never went out of Nashik to any city with Purohit. However, this time Bagde would go out every few minutes to the adjoining room, speak to some senior on the phone, and come back with more queries. Finally, he said, 'You don't know what we can do. We can arrest you right now and make you talk.' He went back to attend one last phone call and returned to tell Joshi that he would have to report to Mumbai ATS right away.

He wasn't even given the opportunity to inform his family at home. They drove straight to Mumbai and reached late night to report at the Kalachowki Police Station, Mumbai ATS office. There they met Dileep Shreerao of the ATS who started with the threat that he could be imprisoned for 15 years if he did not co-operate. Then began the same questions all over again but with many more threats thrown in between. Finally, Shreerao asked him to come clean on the Malegaon blast conspiracy, and Joshi repeated he knew nothing about it nor did he believe Purohit would have anything to do with a terror attack.

On 13 November, he was dropped back at Nashik. His cell phone was also confiscated. However, he hardly got a few hours in Nashik as he was asked to report back to Mumbai once again the same evening when he got his mobile back. Obviously, the ATS had done whatever it needed his mobile for. This time Joshi was taken to a room where Col Purohit was being interrogated. His friend, the decorated Army officer, was made to sit on the dirty floor and constables were interrogating him in the foulest language he had ever heard anywhere. After some minutes, Capt Joshi was told that the same fate awaited him if he did not give up his stance.

Another round of ominous threats. This time Shreerao was joined by the Investigating Officer of the case, Mohan Kulkarni. Kulkarni menacingly told him that they could slap any number of false cases against him, and evidences and witnesses could be 'created' at any time to support those cases. He was then taken to the top floor of the ATS office and put in a dormitory where he spent a sleepless night, and understandably so. Early next morning, Joshi was taken to the office again and made to sit in a room for about three hours. Various persons came and asked him the same questions over and over again. Shreerao also came and told him he would not be able to get away if he didn't co-operate. 'We will get you,' were the ATS officer's words.

In the afternoon, he was taken back to Bhonsala Academy and asked by the accompanying officer, Mr Kanade, to wait for their call. Late in the evening, he got a call from IO Kulkarni, asking him to reach the Nashik ATS office. This time the personnel 'upgraded' their threat and told Joshi that his entire family would be implicated in false cases if he didn't make up his mind now. 'If we can arrest a serving lieutenant colonel and Shankaracharya, we can easily do the same with you and your family members.' Clear as day. Not even an effort at sugar-coating or camouflaging. Faced with the prospect of being implicated in all kinds of cases for the rest of his life and the same fate befalling his family, Capt Nitin Joshi finally put up his hands. He agreed to give a statement as desired. Joshi has narrated that a bat came flying into the room at that moment. ASI Bagde, who had been pro-active in the case from day one, said, 'Look at that bat. It flies when someone is about to die. Looks like your time is up Joshi.' Nobody said anything to that.

Once Joshi had given in, the ATS team did not waste a minute. They started for Mumbai immediately in a police vehicle. Once in Mumbai, IO Kulkarni, along with their accompanying officer Kanade, dictated the statement they wanted recorded under Section 164 in front of a Magistrate. The purport of the statement was that in 2006, Joshi had kept arms and ammunition, given to him by Lt Col Prasad Shrikant Purohit, in his house for a month; that he had seen RDX being hidden in a green sack at Purohit's residence in Deolali; that Purohit, in private conversation, had confessed to him that the RDX was supplied for Samjhauta Express blast; also that Purohit, in early 2008, had told him about something being planned to be done soon, around October/November 2008, somewhere in Nashik district. Further, that in October 2008, a person named Rakesh Dhawade had come to stay in the Bhonsala campus. Joshi was made to say that Purohit sent a boy called Praveen Kumar to Dhawade to learn martial arts and also about weapons and explosives.

As related by him in the complaint made to SHRC, Joshi was reminded several times during the process that he and his family would pay a heavy price if he even thought of retracting his statement. The final shape to the statement was given by Shreerao after telephonic consultation with the late Hemant Karkare. During this period, he spent his nights at a relative's house in Parel where he was guarded round the clock by a constable.

Finally, the recording of his statement before a Magistrate was scheduled on 18 November 2008. At the ATS office, earlier that day, IO Kulkarni pointed a loaded pistol at his forehead and warned that if he ever thought of retracting from the dictated line, one bullet would be enough to blow his brains. On reaching Girgaon Court, another personnel of the Mumbai ATS took him to a corner outside the Magistrate's room and showing a loaded pistol repeated the same threat all over again. On recording his statement, Capt Joshi observed that it was not sealed but just stapled in an envelope. 'It's perfect,' remarked IO Kulkarni. A crestfallen Joshi finally reached his Nashik residence just before dawn on 19 November.

But his ordeal didn't end there. On 30 November, he was called to the Nashik ATS office where he found Kulkarni again who told him menacingly never to think of retracting his statement in court else the consequences would be too costly for his family. The tension and the sinister developments soured Joshi's professional relations with the Bhonsala Academy management and he quit his job within weeks.

Back in Thane, in his private residence, Capt Nitin Dattatray Joshi, who had no other ambitions but to teach young men to serve the country as soldiers, was overcome with remorse. The guilt that he could not stand up for truth despite being an Army officer, and that his statement had implicated a staunch patriot and one of the finest officers he had ever met, eventually did not let Joshi rest. It was at this point that he lodged the complaint with the State Human Rights Commission alleging the human rights abuse he had suffered and to bring the ATS officers to justice.

Statement of Swami Amritanand Dev Tirth

The damning revelations of Subedar Keshav Karbhari Pawar, Major Praveen Khanzode and Capt (retd) Nitin D Joshi are more than enough for a person of average intelligence, capable of putting two and two together, to understand what lay behind the prosecution's strongest 'evidence' against Lt Col PS Purohit. But it would be unfair to miss one more interesting and supporting statement here. The story of the 'confession' of Swami Amritanand Dev Tirth also referred to as Shankaracharya at some places in the case files.

The Swami had given a statement under the provisions of MCOCA to a DCP of the Mumbai Police. However, things changed when he was produced before the Chief Judicial Magistrate. As per procedure, the Judge put some questions to him, and then she wrote in her order that as per the accused, the answers given to questions 10 and 11 were incorrect. He had been coerced to record those statements on the condition that if he gave those answers and turned approver, it would be helpful for him to get an early release in the case. The Judge also allowed him to write in his own hand that he had been falsely implicated in the case.

The questions referred to by the judge were related to Purohit's alleged game plan of carrying out terror strikes at various places.

With these testimonies and details, which are shocking enough to beat any conspiracy shown in sordid web series, I shall move on to what lay in store for Purohit after this formal arrest. Over to the next chapter.

Torture Files

If nothing else sounds convincing, one has to just check out the tortures, both physical and mental, meted out to Lt Col Prasad Shrikant Purohit, a decorated serving officer of the Indian Army. Even the briefest account of these untold tortures, harrowing to say the least, will suffice to give an idea why the perpetrators of the tortures were so desperate to extract confessions from this officer. Why was it so absolutely essential to brand him a terrorist when he was assigned to do exactly the opposite? Who stood to benefit if an Army officer, working in the intelligence wing, was discredited, incarcerated and branded the face of Hindu or Saffron terror?

Questions are many, and one has to forage through multi-layered events and information to get to the bottom of it all. But first, it is pertinent to know what tortures this officer was subjected to. Perhaps, these torture files may help to lift the curtain from the 'real' thing. It would definitely provide a window peep at least.

The Curious Flight to Mumbai

The officers who apprehended Purohit did not even wait for him to leave his premises before embarking on gross violation of basic human rights. While claiming that he had been given 'Movement Orders' from Pachmarhi, Col RK Srivastava compelled Purohit to deposit his phone with the Adjutant there, Lt Col GC Mohanta. In hindsight, we can see that the tortures actually started from that very moment. If his destination was indeed the Integrated Headquarters (MoD) in New Delhi for an interaction with the Military Intelligence-20 as claimed by Col RK Srivastava, what was the need for an officer to leave his cell phone behind? It is pertinent to add that at the time of departure, Purohit had his mother's cell phone as his own mobile had already been taken away on the intervening night of 24-25 October under the pretext of an 'enquiry'. So the phone Purohit deposited with Col Mohanta was actually his mother's. The device was later handed over to his wife by the Adjutant's office. No air tickets were shown to him before flying.

Purohit's suspicions germinated right when his phone was snatched but grew exponentially once he realised at Bhopal airport that he was not being flown to Delhi but Mumbai. Throughout the flight, he was given no convincing answers about the sudden change in plan. At the airport, the check-in was handled by Col Srivastava who also kept the boarding cards firmly in his hands. With no mobile phone, Purohit had no option but to try using a pay-phone to inform his family about being taken to Mumbai. Col Srivastava started showing his high-handedness even before they landed in Mumbai. He asked Purohit to keep silent and threatened physical force if he tried to use the pay-phone.

Mumbai and the Drive to Hell

The team landed in Mumbai close to 2300 hours. Purohit was soon whisked off in a Tata Sumo vehicle to an unknown location outside Mumbai. There was an Intelligence Bureau officer who seemed to guide the team. After a two-hour drive, they arrived at a bungalow which (as he later learnt) was located in Khandala some way off the National Highway. The IB official was one Sanjeev Garg of Mumbai.

The team officers did not waste a single minute after arriving there. The torture saga began almost immediately. Purohit was led into a room with just an entrance and no windows. A team of interrogators awaited him at the cottage. They were ten in number, all from the Anti-Terrorism Squad (ATS) of Mumbai Police, dressed in civvies. The first two hours were just sharp questions and answers with no physical force exerted during the interrogation. But the 'peaceful' couple of hours went by too soon.

By now a sense of helplessness had started taking over the captive army officer. First, the sudden and totally unexplained Movement Order in the middle of a training class, the seizing of his cell phone, the change in destination and above all the inability to contact and inform either his family or even a colleague about all the unexplained things he was being subjected to. The officers around him at the undisclosed location were not only many in number but also senior in terms of service and physical power. In any case, it was foolish to confront them physically.

In his petition to the National Human Rights Commission (NHRC), Lt Col Purohit listed the officers at the Khandala cottage as:

Hemant Karkare, IPS and the then Head of ATS, Mumbai. Notably, Karkare passed away the very next month in a brutal attack when terrorists struck Mumbai on 26-27 November.

With him was Param Bir Singh, IPS and Additional CP, ATS, Mumbai.

We already know Lt Col RK Srivastava and Sanjeev

Garg who joined him at the Mumbai airport.

One un-named CBI officer.

Two or three more Inspector rank officers of ATS, Mumbai.

That, in essence, was the line-up of the personnel who 'dealt with' Col Purohit during the days of his 'illegal confinement' since he was not declared under arrest or in the custody of any agency or police.

In his two petitions sent to the National Human Rights Commission (NHRC), Lt Col Purohit has described in vivid detail the physical and mental tortures he was made to undergo during this period which does not find mention in any of the 'official' files, because, while he was surrounded by top officers round the clock, he wasn't technically arrested by any authority. A copybook case of human rights violation if there was any. I scanned both the petitions from beginning to end in an effort to understand what he went through during those four or five nights and days. One thing stood out very clearly. While the ATS team was headed by Hemant Karkare, and he was present there most of the time, two names led the team in perpetrating the physical tortures as well as mental trauma with their language and behaviour. These were Col RK Srivastava, who had gone all the way to Pachmarhi to escort him, and Param Bir Singh, Additional CP and in practical terms number two in the ATS team. This, again, is borne out by the NHRC petition as well as some inside sources in the Mumbai and Pune circles whom I spoke to.

After an initial round of rather 'tame' questioning, Col Srivastava suddenly pounced on Purohit with a volley of filthy abuses while slapping him and then kicking him all over his body. As if on cue, the constables and a Head Constable of the Mumbai ATS came forward and pinned him on his chair, holding his hands behind his back and pulling his hair back severely so that Srivastava could rain blows on his face. After raining blows on his face, Srivastava again kicked him with his shoes on.

Param Bir Singh, who was watching from afar until then, now swung into action. While Col Srivastava stood on the captive's feet rendering him totally immobile and numbed, Param Bir started kicking and slapping. By now, Purohit's shirt was removed and trousers lowered. With his feet pressed down with boots and hands tied behind the chair, he had no way to protect himself from the blows. Displaying a harrowing sadistic streak, Param Bir started twisting Purohit's nipples and pulling off hair from his chest. As the victim bore the untold pain, his private parts were also pulled and twisted repeatedly, making him, as he wrote in his petition, 'face hell and nothing else but hell'. The beating, kicking, twisting of private parts, and pulling off hair went on unhindered for five more days. With no way of contacting anyone and no access to any legal or official recourse of any kind,

Col Purohit felt completely broken by the end of those five-six days.

The ordeal would go on till almost 3 November, the day before Purohit would be moved back to Mumbai. The tortures, of course, were to continue for a much longer time. During his confinement at the Khandala bungalow, Karkare limited himself to vile abuses and threats while watching his men, Param Bir Singh and the two Inspectors, try third-degree tortures on a serving army officer. Meanwhile, on 2 November, Col Srivastava came up with the idea of handcuffing the captive so that they need not tie his hands behind the chair. So handcuffs it was. Finally, Purohit had a brief respite when he was moved from the bungalow late in the afternoon on 4 November to be taken back to Mumbai.

All through these nightmarish days, the sole thrust of Karkare, Param Bir, Col Srivastava and the other personnel was to pressurise Purohit to own up to the Malegaon blasts. Towards the end of the fifth day, Col Srivastava tried his *Brahmastra*[14] by threatening his brother officer that he would parade Purohit's mother, sister and wife naked in front of him if he refused to own up to the blasts. Purohit shuddered because by now he was convinced that these officers were capable of carrying out any abominable threat.

---

14 *Brahmastra*: The ultimate weapon that exists during a battle

I also read in the petition that the team of Hemant Karkare, Param Bir Singh and Col Srivastava tried another trick. They would loudly discuss in his presence how they could plant explosives either in Purohit's ancestral home or at his army quarters. This again jolted the captive army officer as he had had no opportunity or means to contact anyone in his family even once. Despite all of it, he did not give in.

Torture Files: Season Two

The tortures, humiliation and threats were in for a break as the ATS team moved Lt Col Purohit back to Mumbai where he was finally shown as 'arrested'. This happened on 5 November 2008. Purohit would learn of his 'formal' arrest only when he heard Inspector Kadam inform his wife in the morning that her husband was under arrest as an accused in a terror conspiracy. But if he had any hopes that the formal arrest would bring an end to the tortures or excesses, those were belied as soon as he was put in custody. In fact, what was to unfold in the next few weeks was the stuff of web series and fiction tales on how to conduct torture sessions if one wants to break the spirit of a tough and self-respecting human being. The 'sessions' started the very next day at the Kalachowki police station which was also the hub of the ATS, Mumbai. Purohit was taken to a room (adjoining the 'official' lock-up room) which had no windows and was totally sound-proof. It had an air conditioner though. Now picture this.

To the left of the room's entrance, placed close to the wall was a 'U' angle embedded upside down on the floor with the help of concrete, etcetera. In a straight line from it, but about eight feet apart was another 'U' angle fixed in the other corner of the room. The officers present told the Colonel to strip down to his underwear, putting the AC at the lowest possible temperature. He was slapped, boxed and humiliated with abuses by Arun Khanvilkar. Khanvilkar then ordered a few junior personnel of the ATS to beat up Purohit black and blue, all the while provoking them saying, 'see how it feels to beat up a colonel of the Indian Army'.

Now started the real tortures which perhaps surpassed all limits of inhumanity. Purohit was made to sit on the floor at a point between the two 'U' angles. Long ropes were tied to his ankles with the other end of the ropes made to pass through the U angles and his legs were stretched out with an inhuman pull. He was almost stretched out at 180 degrees but was being compelled to sit up with his back erect by one personnel constantly kicking and forcing him from behind. This put intolerable pressure on his thighs and groins sending a shooting pain first in his limbs and then the entire body. Unable to bear the excruciating pain, he soon fainted. But every time he passed out, the ATS personnel shocked him into waking up by pouring cold water on him in the freezing air-conditioned room.

There was more to come. The next round of tortures included beating on the palms and feet with a big-sized bell just like those strung in temples. All the time, he was laid out on the floor with his legs stretched between the U angles. The torture sessions were mostly being 'overseen' by Khanvilkar and his colleague, Mohan Kulkarni, who was the Investigating Officer of the case. Purohit pleaded that he had been operated upon thrice in his right knee and had a ligament reconstruction surgery with an implant fixed with two screws. Hence, his knees and thighs were in no position to undergo such tortures. His pleadings, in fact, had a contrary effect. Knowing that his limbs were vulnerable, the men scaled up the beatings and the torturous 'stretching'. Overcome with pain and almost numbed to the core, Purohit lost count of days. On the fourth or fifth day, his right knee swelled up like a balloon. Only then did the stretching sessions stop as the officers perhaps realised that this could result in a medical emergency and thus invite undue attention. But that did not mean the ATS had turned human or even considerate. This was, at best, a change of tactics. Both Khanvilkar and Kulkarni put their heads together and came up with something new.

They got an iron pipe fixed on the corner opposite to the entrance of the same room at a height of about eight to ten feet from the floor. Purohit was stripped naked, his wrists were tied with ropes to the pipe and he was made to dangle from the pipe with his feet hanging above the ground. Now hold your breath.

A constable would stand behind Purohit holding a thick log at his waist level. Another, on orders from Param Bir Singh, Arun Khanvilkar or Mohan Kulkarni or all three, would pull the ropes tied to his ankles with a great force and then release them suddenly making him bang against the log with tremendous force causing a terrible impact on his lower back and waist. This latest torture formula continued for at least another three days.

As for the vile abuses and threats, there was no limit. Mohan Kulkarni was the most foul-mouthed in his abuses about the women of Purohit's family, but every time the latter reacted, he was brutally slapped and beaten up for it. It was during this custody period that Col Purohit was taken to Bangalore for a Narco-analysis test. On return, he learnt that his father-in-law and lawyer had obtained permission from the court to meet him. Till then, he had not seen anyone else except Col Srivastava and the ATS and police personnel.

By then, Gujarat, Andhra Pradesh and Haryana police had also landed in Mumbai. They started their own round of questioning and threats, tying to pressurise Purohit to own up to the Hyderabad Mecca Masjid and the Samjhauta Express blasts respectively. In the midst of one of these sessions (on return from Bangalore), Purohit was suddenly accosted by Khanvilkar who barged into the room, slapped him hard and then threatened that he would be eliminated in an encounter if he so much as uttered a word about the tortures he was being subjected to. Officials of Andhra Pradesh and Haryana Police parroted the same threats from their side. When Purohit was finally taken to meet his father-in-law and lawyer, Khanvilkar and Col Srivastava were already present in the room. The inmate was allowed all of five minutes to speak to his visitors. Those precious five minutes were hardly sufficient even to just enquire about the wellbeing of his family, leave alone share any details. The moment the visitors were shown out, Col Srivastava came threateningly to Purohit and started abusing him. As per the recorded details in his complaint, Srivastava said, 'Purohit, I promise you, very soon your mother, wife and sister will also be put behind bars, and henceforth your sons will grow up in some orphanage.' Purohit's protest against involving the family at every stage was met by another round of brutal thrashing and kicking.

On 24 November 2008 or about three weeks since he was 'picked up' from Pachmarhi, Purohit mustered up the courage to raise the issues related to his physical condition at the MCOCA court in Mumbai Sessions. Upon which, the court referred him to the Military Hospital, INHS Asvini in Colaba, Mumbai. After various tests, medical reports confirmed the tortures and trauma outlined in the above paragraphs.

His illegal detention between 29 October and 4 November, as well as the illegal tortures, formed the basis of two petitions to the National Human Rights Commission as well as two back-to-back internal enquiries by the Army. While the Army Court of Inquiry's papers are out of bounds for most people except a select few, the NHRC petition served to bring out the brutalities that Lt Col Purohit was undergoing. It also made the world outside somewhat aware of the bizarre sequence of events which occurred from Pachmarhi to Mumbai. Of course, the beatings and tortures caused permanent damage to his knees, which still hinders him in his activities. The injuries also led to long-term complications in his elbows, wrists and palms. But if the end purpose of all the brutalities was getting him to 'confess' to the blasts, that certainly did not happen, and Col Purohit (like so many others in the case) continues to fight it out in the law courts.

The Better Half

First Shocker

It was a lazy autumn afternoon in Pachmarhi. Aparna Purohit, a practising homeopath, was taking life easy for once. In order to take care of her younger son who was just a toddler then, and make the most of her husband's posting in Pachmarhi, she had opted for a break from treating patients and enrolled herself in a psychotherapy study programme to enhance her professional prospects.

As all the phones in her residence suddenly started ringing non-stop, she rushed to check what was causing so much activity. On answering the phone, she was asked to watch the news on television. As she switched on the TV set, she saw shrieking headlines 'breaking' the news about the Mumbai ATS arresting a serving army colonel for no less than engineering a terror attack.

At first, she just felt curious because she was under the impression that her husband was in Delhi as per the movement orders. This was the evening of November 01. However, the news flashes gave her a nagging feeling. So, she went to the Adjutant's office the next morning (November 02) to check if all was well. The Adjutant, Col Mohanta, did not share the location but assured her that her husband was with the army and there was nothing to worry. Another day passed. On November 03, she got a phone call from a common contact in the army in Mumbai who hinted that her husband was in Mumbai, not Delhi, and expressed some apprehension about the latter's safety.

Aparna tried to check once more with the local office but there was no update. She prayed that all would be well. Another day passed without any news or phone call from her husband. It was finally on the morning of November 05 that her worst fears came true when an ATS officer informed her on the phone that her husband had been arrested. He did not specify on what charge but told her that they would be producing him before a Magistrate shortly. Not knowing who else to turn to in such an unprecedented situation, she rushed to the Adjutant's office once more demanding to know what this was all about. She was pretty sure it was nothing but confusion at some level. Why would Prasad be named in a terror case unless there was some serious misinformation, she argued. An intelligent woman herself, Aparna was pretty well aware of the nature of her husband's job and the fact that covert operations were an integral part of his assignment. Hence, she was quite convinced that this was nothing more than someone 'misinforming' or 'misleading' the ATS about some operations, thus causing this whole fiasco. She assured herself that this would all be sorted out in a few days at the most. The Adjutant too did not seem to have much clarity on the situation until then, and he asked her to go home while he made the necessary enquiries. He apparently assured her that it had to be a misunderstanding of some sort. But despite his assuring thoughts, Aparna could not relax. She insisted she would not get up from the Adjutant's office, till she had managed to find out all there was to learn. Finally, the office was able to gather from the headquarters in Nashik that Col Purohit was indeed in the custody of the Anti-Terrorism Squad, because he had been found involved in conspiring and engineering the Malegaon Blast. Trying her best to process this crisis that had befallen her in a matter of hours, Aparna trudged back home to break the news to the kids before someone else fed their version to them. The younger one, just a toddler, wasn't old enough to understand anything more than the fact that Baba was going to be away for some days. But the older one had watched the television flashes and needed explaining.

November set in. Aparna needed to gather her support system, but as God would have it, her parents were abroad then. It took them some time to cut short their visit and return to India. Other relatives, of course, contacted her, but nobody really knew how to help in such a situation. Suddenly news came that Purohit would be produced in the Nashik court and then taken away to Mumbai. Aparna immediately called up her maternal uncle, who lived in Nashik, to somehow reach out to the ATS team there. He was able to catch up with Col Purohit for just a few minutes and that too only when he was brought in to be produced in the court. She had had no communication with him at all. And what her *Mama* (maternal uncle) conveyed, gave her little consolation. If anything, it created further confusion because she still could not process intelligently all that had happened in those first few days.

It is a no-brainer that in any crisis a wife would side with her husband and give him the benefit of doubt even if the whole world differed. But in Aparna Purohit's case, it was not just about a wife trusting her spouse. It went much beyond. In the absence of anyone coming to the support of the family, she rose to the occasion and became the anchor in Col Purohit's fight. All of Purohit's friends, including the lawyers, credit Aparna for conquering her inner fears and giving a direction to the legal fight. It would not be an exaggeration to say that though it was the lawyers who argued in the courtroom, Purohit's real lawyer was Aparna. But before she plunged herself into the relentless battle, the soft spoken but resolute woman had to first conquer her own demons.

As is often the case in most Indian families, the relatives and friends were circumspect about speaking honestly to her. Firstly, they themselves had little idea of what was actually going on. Secondly, those colleagues and friends who did understand the gravity of the situation didn't have the heart to tell her in so many words. It is in such dire circumstances that someone comes forward with the courage to 'break' the news. And sometimes, as one of my lawyer friends would say, shake you by the collar to make you see things as they are. In Aparna's case, this crucial role was played by her first cousin. As her brother too was abroad, she contacted her cousin for help. He told her in clear terms that there was nothing left for her in Pachmarhi, and she needed to get back to Mumbai for the sake of the children and her own safety. At the time of the arrest, the Purohits' elder son was six plus whereas the younger one was just a toddler. On her cousin's advice, Aparna stayed in Mumbai till such time her husband was in custody in Nashik. Only when he was shifted to Mumbai did she move to live with her relatives in Pune, though most of her weekdays were spent travelling between Mumbai and Pune. But we will come to that shortly.

So, as soon she as came to Mumbai, her cousin, whose name she wasn't keen on sharing, told her clearly that her continuing to stay in Pachmarhi was nothing but her denial to accept the stark reality in front of her. As things stood, she should stop hoping for it to be 'business as usual' anytime soon, he underscored. He also added that, going by the indications, she might have to do a lot of running around which would require a support system that was only possible where the rest of the extended family was available. At one stage, when she resisted, he literally scolded her into seeing things 'as they were'. Interestingly, his clinching argument was, no matter how false or drummed-up the case, this was after all a case of terror conspiracy and not likely to get sorted anytime soon even if (and this was a big if) things went as per plan. In hindsight, we know now that things didn't go as per plan at all. But still, Aparna recalled to me in her own words, despite her cousin's scolding, she didn't quite come to terms with the reality completely. Of course, it made her realise the gravity of the situation, but she continued to think that whatever the 'misunderstanding' it would be cleared out in the courts with help from the army in a matter of few weeks or a couple of months at the most.

However, moving to Mumbai did jolt her enough to get down to the practical challenges. The first of these challenges was to engage a competent lawyer who would be ready to take up the unprecedented brief of a decorated serving officer being accused of terror. She found one in Shrikant Shivade whose first job was to explain to her the rights of a person or detainee in these circumstances. Until then, Aparna did not even have an idea that the detained person had certain rights which his family could and should invoke. In fact, the next eight or nine years of her life were going to be like enrolling in a law school except the classes would be held in real life instead of a law school building.

Many weeks had passed by then, but Aparna had not had even a glimpse of her husband. That opportunity finally came when he was being produced in court for the third time. In her own words, 'I can never forget that day in my life and that look of Prasad that I saw in court.' Never had she seen him so depressed or dishevelled or perhaps even disoriented. But Aparna recalled that what had hurt her most during that fleeting first interaction was her husband not looking her straight in the eye. In fact, he did not speak anything and refused to respond to her at all. In hindsight, it became clear that this was what the weeks of physical and mental tortures, coercions and threats had done to the personality of a brave, intelligent and dedicated officer. For some unexplained reason, lawyer Shivade also asked her not to force him to talk. So Aparna sat silently while the lawyer discussed some essential legal issues with her prisoner husband. The conversation with the lawyer, which was purely technical, appeared to have boosted his confidence, and when he was leaving the court, his expression was 'a shade better' than it was when entering. Perhaps it was his way of coming to terms with the shattering travesty that he was now facing his family as a terror accused, an enemy of the nation when all he had ever done was talk about his love for the country and his passion to weed out the enemies.

Col Purohit's appearance had shaken Aparna to the core. But it had an interesting impact on the overall situation, particularly, from the long-term perspective. The distraught, disoriented look and the avoiding eyes of her husband finally jolted Aparna out of the stupor which even her cousin's harsh scolding had not quite succeeded in doing. She realised that waiting around for things to come back on track was not going to work. That was the day, Aparna Purohit, a low-profile homeopath, pursuing a psychotherapy course, mother of two, decided she had to take matters in her own hands and do whatever was possible within her means to fight out the 'misunderstanding' against her husband. Even then, the idea that this could be a conspiracy hadn't occurred to Aparna. She still stuck to her view that a misunderstanding caused in one of her husband's covert operations must have led to this situation, but since it was now entangled in legal complications, it might require a longer legal battle. Her idea of 'longer' was still two or three months.

Though nobody in the family or friends' circle of Prasad Purohit, much less his wife, had any inkling that he would be languishing in jail for the next nine years, at least she pulled up her socks that very day and decided to immerse herself in the legal battle as far as her means would permit. Meanwhile, Purohit had now been shifted to Pune and that made things a bit more convenient. At least in terms of meeting. With their lawyer's support, Aparna was now able to meet her husband on a regular basis in jail. Those 'jail sessions' turned out be yet another learning experience, both legally as well as in life.

The Jailbird

With regular visits to the jail, sometimes to sort out legal issues and at other times just to chat and keep up her husband's spirits, Aparna found herself becoming a part of a completely new world – the world of inmates' families. A world which had its own dynamics, its own rules-regulations and its own fears and triumphs; where getting a few minutes extra time with your family member was like a blessing and losing out on the chance to meet. a great disappointment, especially if you had travelled a long distance to reach the jail premises. While she waited for hours for her turn to meet, Aparna said, there was nothing to do but observe the family members who came to meet various inmates and get a peep into their world. It gave her an opportunity to know the plight of people who were languishing as under trials for years and years without any hope of redemption whatsoever. As mentioned above, it opened her eyes to a completely new world, one which common middle-class Indians never even thought of, unless pushed by fate.

But that wasn't all. As she almost became a 'jailbird' herself, the exposure to the other inmates' families helped her in another significant way. By learning about the plight of so many others, it finally started sinking in that contrary to her calculations, this ordeal was certainly not going to end in a few months. With each passing visit, this was getting clearer and clearer. And that was when she finally pulled up her socks for the long haul. We will come to that shortly.

But while discussing the jail visits with Aparna, what struck me most was how vividly she remembered the minutest details of the place. Her powers of observation, as well as her impeccable memory, was amazing. From what I gathered from our brief conversations, her life had almost 'settled' into a routine which mostly involved commuting between her home, jail and the lawyers' chambers. It went something like this....

On meeting days, she would report at the jail office by 9:30 in the morning and submit her application along with the relevant documents every time. By noon, she would be informed whether her meeting was likely to happen or not, depending on the number of other applicants.

Her turn could come anytime till early evening though the actual meeting with Lt Col Purohit could never be stretched beyond ten minutes. In other words, she had to devote an entire day for those ten-odd minutes. But one shudders to think what more could have gone wrong had she not immersed herself completely in the legal and psychological fight for her incarcerated husband.

Those ten-odd minutes that she usually managed after a day-long wait could hardly qualify as 'conversation' though. First there was the challenge of keeping one's voice low. Considering the sensitive nature of the details, she was always wary of other people, who were chatting in the adjacent windows, listening-in. On top of that, the use of the 'across window' telephone was a huge dampener. It was difficult to discuss details that way, and the time was never enough. Finally, the Purohits found a workable solution for this. Aparna would come to every 'meeting' armed with a list of details that were wanted by the lawyer to prepare his brief. She would hand them over in her short meeting. Col Purohit would then utilise the time till the next meeting to jot down all the details in small slips of paper. Most of the time, it included detailing of the sequence of events as they had unfolded to clarify his position. It was then Aparna's job to come back home, write down the details in a coherent manner, type them on the computer and pass them on to the lawyer who could use them accordingly. Soon, her involvement in the actual legal affairs of the case was set to become much deeper.

Gradually, she started sitting with the lawyer in his office and became hands-on in preparing the brief based on the details provided by her husband. She would sit on the computer, typing out pages upon pages almost becoming a part of his legal team.

The First Taste of Victory

In the initial months, Aparna Purohit would attend every court hearing with a lot of hope. Her hopes rested mainly on the fact that, hearing after hearing, the prosecution was able to prove nothing against her husband. And yet, there were no tangible results. It was after a painful two long years, with many ups and downs, that she and her lawyer Shrikant Shivade decided that there was no way it could get solved in the lower courts. And that was when they started seeking help from other senior lawyers and moved courts at a higher level. But before we get to that, it is essential to mention one turning point which not only brought the first ray of hope for the family but also compelled people for the first time to reflect on the case with a new perspective. It compelled a lot of people to think 'afresh' on the entire case and consider that perhaps things may not be as they were made out to be.

In 2009, a couple of months before the first anniversary of Col Purohit's arrest, the court dropped the

MCOCA charges on all accused in the case. This came as a major jolt to the ATS as they knew that things would not be the same for them henceforth.

Here is what the *Times of India* team of reporters said under the headline 'Court Drops MCOCA Against Sadhvi, Purohit'

> The Anti-Terrorism Squad (ATS) of the Maharashtra Police suffered a setback in Malegaon blast case on Friday when a special court in Mumbai dropped all charges under the Maharashtra Control of Organised Crime Act (MCOCA) against 11 suspects including former army man (sic) Lt Col Prasad Shrikant Purohit and Sadhvi Pragya Singh Thakur.

The *Times of India* report further read,

> The dropping of charges means that the accused will no longer face trial under the stringent law and their case will be sent back to a regular court in Nashik. As long as MCOCA was applicable to the case, the prosecution enjoyed a considerable advantage as it could use confessions given by the accused to police as evidence. The decision to strike down MCOCA may also make it easier for the accused to get bail.

This report was filed in the *Times of India* on 2 August

2009. Of course, we know now that despite the dropping of MCOCA, it would take another seven years before the accused got bail. As for the use of the terms 'former' or 'ex' army man for Col Purohit, it was common those days, since media persons appeared confused about his official status. Most people, including journalists, were under the impression that he had been sacked. Nobody cared to check that he was still a serving officer.

It must be mentioned here that the MCOCA order was challenged in the High Court and arguments went on for a long time. Eventually Aparna, their lawyer and the entire legal team realised the futility of these unending arguments and sittings.

Meanwhile, the High Court rejected bail to Purohit. Neela Gokhale, a senior lawyer in the Supreme Court and close friend of the family, was also involved in Col Purohit's case. It was she who took the initiative and pressed the Purohits to move the Supreme Court. Gokhale was also instrumental in getting one of India's best known legal minds Harish Salve to represent Purohit in the apex court for the bail plea. Salve's presence generated some expected media attention. It also made things a little difficult for the prosecution. We will discuss in detail about how Salve argued the case in a separate chapter. But suffice it to say here that on the basis of the Army's internal Court of Inquiry findings and as Salve himself underlined 'the untenability of the evidence', he was able to secure bail with his clinching arguments.

The media went into a tizzy soon after. Aparna was almost mobbed for her comments. She tried her best to keep her composure in order to co-ordinate with the legal team and fulfil the required formalities, but the physical and emotional strain was bound to overwhelm anyone in her situation. The slow and almost static pace was suddenly taken over by the fast moving events. There was much paper work to be done at the Mumbai and Pune levels. Aparna was required to stay back in Delhi for a couple of more days to tie up a few loose ends. Exactly two days later, on 23 August 2017, her incarcerated husband would see the light of day, nine years after living inside dark cells in various jails, not knowing if he would ever come out.

The day the Supreme Court granted bail to Col Purohit, there were hours and hours of loud, acrimonious debates in all Hindi, English and most regional language news channels. And not just on that day. From that day in the Supreme Court lawns, right till the day he came out, his bail order, the role of ATS and its failure to present a water-tight case, and by default the entire set of cases billed as Hindu terror were not only top news but the only subject of debate in news channels and newspaper analyses.

Here, I am particularly reminded of one such television show. NDTV, which had been tracking the case like so many others, devoted an entire prime time debate that evening to discussing why an army escort was sent to receive Purohit when he came out of the Taloja Jail. Panellists outshouted each other in arguing that Purohit needed to be protected as there was threat to his life while another set of panellists condemned the army's move to provide security and escort to a terror accused. This is just to give a glimpse of the kind of micro media debating that went on and also what kind of questions were raised to keep the issue alive.

To be sure, a lot of channels also raised pointed questions at the ATS – the travesty of a serving military officer arrested on terror charges, kept in jail for nine long years and then released on bail with many conditions, because the concerned agency had not been able to substantiate the charges to the court's satisfaction.

Elder One Grows up too Soon, the Little One hit the Hardest

Common contacts, sources and my own research had given me a fair idea of the courage, resilience and efforts of Aparna Purohit. But the calm, composure and relative objectivity with which she discussed everything from scratch, still came as a surprise. Whether it was the humiliation, the legal tangles or her own fight with the circumstances, she was able to narrate it all, almost from a third person's perspective. If there was ever a moment when her voice faltered and she became tongue-tied, it was while sharing the experiences of her youngest born, the second son who was no more than a toddler when his father was taken away.

It was clear within minutes of our conversation that the little one had been hit the hardest by the turn of events which rocked the Purohit family. It was also clear that while she fought an unending legal battle and the social stigma attached with the whole case, she wasn't as perturbed by those battles as she was by the devastating impact it all had on her younger son. While the elder Purohit boy turned somewhat into a loner and internalised the whole thing, thus becoming a young man who was too mature for his age, the younger one perhaps didn't really know how to react to all that was happening around.

His initial reactions started with the media frenzy in the first few weeks of his father's arrest. The constant media crews following the family and the non-stop news coverage was like a whirlpool, and the family seemed to be getting sucked into it with the little one perhaps the most perplexed with it all. To take control of things, Aparna implemented the unwritten rule that no news channels would be watched in the household. Headlines were a strict no-no. This, of course, only had a partial impact because neighbours, friends and schoolmates were always there to enquire about the case and remind the family of the details they picked up from the media. Despite the challenges and her absences, Aparna tried, like any other mother, to keep the conversation and mood in the house as normal as circumstances would permit. The repeated shifting also did not help. In her own words, the running of the household or looking after her sons per se wasn't such a challenge. She had her mother-in-law, her elder sister-in-law, and her own parents also did their bit. The family allowed her all the time and space to do the running around and the travelling for the legal battles. The children had already been shifted from their school in Pachmarhi to Pune so that the family could be together. She was spared the day-to-day worries of food, schooling, exams, etcetera. But even when she was in Pune, she had to spend long hours with the lawyer and his team and often came home late, physically and mentally exhausted. However, it was not the day-to-day care of the kids which worried her so much as the psychological impact of the circumstances.

Her worries were further aggravated, when, long after the unwritten ban on news channels at home, she found her elder son collecting headlines and newspaper cuttings of stories related to his father. Another day, she was pained to find him in their library looking for definition of 'bail'. That was the time when bail hearings were going on in the court. She confided in me that although her elder son avoided discussing the case or even asking a single question for fear of upsetting her, he was definitely 'processing' it all in his own mind. Perhaps his over-seriousness and long hours of silence were also a result of the same 'processing'. She had no way of knowing what was going on in his mind but very soon her young innocent son was to become a compatriot in her struggle as he started helping her out with the paper work.

Initially, it was just to jot down the prison notes and type them out for legal reference. But gradually he picked up the finer points and helped her substantially in drafting letters, writing applications and all other kinds of paperwork. By the time he was in high school, the elder Purohit boy had become his mother's biggest associate in the struggle for his father. Something even legal eagles found difficult to digest.

But it was a very different story with the little one. The child who was just a toddler reacted in a very adverse way to the whole affair. His complications started soon after his father was taken away. He was constantly irritable and reactive to everyone. Being too young to understand the situation in its right perspective, he started reacting the only way kids of his age do...by throwing tantrums. His irritation and tantrums reached a peak whenever he met his father in court during the hearings. Seeing him confused with all that was going on around him, Aparna decided it was important to have a clear conversation with the child before he drew his own conclusions. So she made him sit with her one day and explained in as simple words as possible about what was happening to his father. He did pretend to understand, but that did not make things any simpler for him or the family.

Aparna, who was studying psychotherapy for professional interest, was able to understand the child's reaction to the strange turn of events. With a mother's instinct and some knowledge of psychology, she managed to channelize his energies. However, he did take to binge eating and irritable behaviour from time to time.

Even though charges under MCOCA were dropped, the bail hearings had failed to bring any relief. The bail for the accused was rejected in the Bombay High Court. The family and the lawyers were now burning the midnight oil to seek bail from the Supreme Court. The mother had to travel too often to Delhi.

Meanwhile, her elder son had moved to a hostel for academic reasons. This had a twin effect on the already harassed family. The younger one, who used to have some fun in his elder brother's company, had now lost his only support and looked for solace in food all his waking hours. His loneliness increased thus making him even more irritable and broody.

As for Aparna, though she never really worried about her elder son, his shifting to the hostel did upset her a bit. Challenges and unexpected circumstances also have a bearing on our relationships in life. In a strange way,

Aparna had begun to depend on her son for support. With his shifting to the hostel, both she and her younger son felt the absence of the older boy in their respective ways.

The day Col Purohit came home after nine years, following the bail order, her younger son's happiness knew no bounds. Aparna recalled his excitement with a lot of joy. The family had been scattered on the day the Supreme Court granted bail to the army officer. Aparna, of course, was in Delhi. The sons were in Pune, but the elder one was in the hostel. Her sister-in-law picked up the younger one from school and gave him the good news. But before she could bring him home, a huge media contingent had already gathered at the Purohit's residence. The protective aunt then decided to take him to a relative's house, because she was scared the child would be mobbed by the media teams. The next day they travelled to Mumbai to await Purohit's release.

But most memorable, in Aparna's own words, are the excited conversations her younger son had with his school mates when the father returned with them to Pune. Without allowing him even a quick break, the son insisted on calling up all his school friends one by one. After updating them about his dad's return, the child pressed Purohit to talk at least a few sentences with each one of his friends. Funny as it may sound, Purohit spoke to each of those kids on the phone, assuring them that he indeed was the father of their friend and would now be around. Deep down in his mind, the kid had been suffering the complex of an absent father while all his friends came to school or went for outings and played games with their dads. Ever since he joined school, he had not had the opportunity to 'show' his dad to anyone. In their own innocent way, children must have asked him questions which he had been unable to answer.

Now that Col Purohit is back, he manages to meet his sons frequently, but Aparna still worries about the younger one because in her own words 'certain reactions become part of one's personality'. The older one, of course, is now a tall and handsome young man and almost on his own. Interestingly, the younger one is all geared up for a career in the forces. Whether this is because of or despite his childhood is something only an expert psychologist would be able to decipher.

The Salve Perspective

After pursuing the story for more than two years, I had managed to speak to several people who knew Lt Col Prasad Shrikant Purohit well. Some professionally, some personally and some others both. Of course, most of them were not ready to be quoted, particularly those who were still serving. Understandably so. Even those who had retired from service tried to give me some excuse or other to wriggle out. More than anything, I was looking for that legal perspective which was needed to throw light on the maze of events and claims-counterclaims. It had to be someone who understood both law and politics. And above all, was not cagey in speaking his mind or always trying to be 'politically correct'. So I tried to catch up with one of India's leading legal luminaries Harish Salve. After all, it was Salve's astute observation and incisive argumentative skills that shredded through the prosecution and got the bail for Col Purohit in 2017.

As it turned out, contacting Mr Salve and getting some candid answers from him was much easier than all the others put together – both military and civilian. Though I was disappointed with the clipped length of the answers, I couldn't complain as he was communicating straight from London. Let me paraphrase some of the answers he gave to my questions and also his very brief but very enlightening remarks on the 'status' of the evidence. Here goes....

To begin at the beginning, I was curious about his first reaction or his first thoughts when he was contacted by Col Purohit's legal team. I asked him how he felt considering the fact that Purohit and others were accused in terror cases.

Harish Salve's answer was brief but telling. He replied, 'Was always sceptical of the Hindu terror narrative for various reasons.... So (I) decided to give it a look.'

So Salve, like so many other Indians who may not be as articulate, had his doubts about the Hindu terror theory from day one. Even though he may have been contacted by the legal team of the accused much later.

His next statement, in answer to my second question, was slightly more detailed and definitely more headline-worthy. I asked him if it wasn't slightly 'out of the way' for a person like him, India's leading legal luminary, to accept a brief for a terror accused. He could possibly have passed it on to someone else or something like that. He replied that 'all accused were entitled to their day in court'. He drew parallels here with the Talwars case, then said that 'on seeing the record' he was convinced that Purohit was being made a 'scapegoat in a battle between political parties'.

So from just the first two queries and the briefest answers, two things became abundantly clear. First, that for someone like Salve, a widely respected nationalist and ace lawyer, the Hindu terror theory had appeared to be a bogus one always. Second, that Col Purohit (among others) could be paying the price for coming in the crosshairs of a far bigger and sinister game being played between political parties. For what reasons we do not know.

Seeing how candid he was about the case, I tried to probe further. The obvious next question was: what exactly did he find on examining the evidence built up against Purohit, and how did he plan to demolish them?

While Harish Salve didn't quite discuss the details of the evidence with me, he was pretty upfront about his conclusions. 'I remember seeing the evidence and realising its untenability,' he told me. Without pointing at the specifics, he said his remarks were based on two very 'important pointers'. The two pointers he indicated were the NIA report and the fact that the Army, after a long and thorough inquiry, had 'not' taken action against Purohit.

On the Army not taking any action on Purohit after the two exhaustive Courts of Inquiry, we have gone through the details in earlier chapters.

But what is the NIA report that the senior counsel was referring to? Well, after much running around and phone calls to 'known' sources, I did manage to read the relevant paragraphs from the NIA charges on which Harish Salve seemed to have based his opinion.

So what did the NIA report actually say?

It said that the 'house of accused Sudhakar Chaturvedi was searched in the presence of Assistant Chemical Analyser, and one detonator, gunny bag etcetera were seized. The samples on cotton swabs were taken from his house and sent to FSL, Mumbai. The report of FSL, Mumbai stated that the seized articles/swabs contained traces of Cyclonite (RDX), Ammonium and Nitrate radicals. FSL has further opined that the explosive ingredients (RDX, Ammonium and Nitrate Radicals) detected in blast site exhibits at Malegaon are similar to the samples seized from the house of accused Sudhakar Chaturvedi.'

The above is an extract from the NIA report.

But the most important evidence comes in the following paragraph of the NIA charge-sheet which appeared as para no 7 in the document.

Para 7 says...

> 'However, during investigation by NIA, it was revealed that Army authorities had conducted a Court of Inquiry against accused Prasad Purohit. As such the proceedings of this Court of Inquiry against accused Prasad Purohit were obtained. During scrutiny of proceedings of COI, it came to light that, X and Y revealed a new fact with regard to the story of assembling of IED in the house of accused Sudhakar Chaturvedi. As such it was decided to re-examine X and examine Y with regard to their deposition in the COI. Therefore, both the officers were examined and they revealed that on 3rd November, 2008 they suspiciously found API in the house of Sudhakar Chaturvedi when the accused Sudhakar Chaturvedi was not present in his house. Both the witnesses, X and Y, confirmed this fact during their examination.'

From the previous chapters, we know that the API here is Assistant Police Inspector Bagde. The names of the witnesses referred to in the report are being held back for understandable reasons.

The NIA report goes on to explain...

'On considering the facts narrated by above mentioned witnesses, the question arises here as to why API Bagde visited the house of Sudhakar Chaturvedi in the absence of accused/witnesses and why he requested XYZ not to tell anything about his presence at the house of Sudhakar Chaturvedi. It is pertinent to mention here that the ATS conducted the search of the house of Sudhakar Chaturvedi on 25/11/2008 from where they had taken the swabs of the RDX. This creates doubts on this recovery of swabs of RDX keeping in view of (sic) the depositions of X and Y. The deposition of X and Y brings to doubt the evidentiary value of the FSL report indicating presence of the traces of RDX in the swabs taken from the house of Sudhakar Chaturvedi during search of his house. This recovery itself becomes suspect on the ground that the ATS Mumbai may have planted the RDX traces to implicate him and other accused persons in the case.'

The remarks above are quoted exactly from the NIA charge-sheet and form part of the legal file in the trial court. The last few sentences are unambiguous in stating that the NIA found merit in the Army's Court of Inquiry at least so far as the 'planting' of RDX, as claimed by Col Purohit, goes. Then, the obvious question is: what remains of the terror charge against the army officer if the RDX argument doesn't hold anymore? Of course, one needs to wait and see how the trial progresses and if and when the courts take cognizance of the argument.

That brings me to the next question I put to Harish Salve. I specifically asked him that in all these years, agencies had not been able to prove their case against Col Purohit despite the voluminous charge-sheets. Did he think this lent some credence to the allegations of conspiracy in the case?

The counsel's reply was thought-provoking. He said, 'There was an unfortunate incident, and there must be some guilty of the act that caused the incident.' Of course, referring to the Malegaon bomb blast. But he added, 'The trouble is when politics around such incidents become overwhelming, then the investigators sometimes lose focus (or are made to lose focus) and concentrate on finding some persons guilty instead of finding those who "are" guilty. This imperils the trial'.

I quote this answer verbatim from our conversation. A couple of very pertinent points can be discerned from his remarks. One, the ATS seemed to be conducting its 'investigation' in a pre-determined direction. Two, politics was driving the investigation from the very beginning though by whom specifically and at what level was left unsaid by the legal eagle.

The obvious question that arose from his reply was, if

indeed he felt politics was driving the investigators, who could it be.

So I asked him…

Who, in your opinion, was or could be behind the conspiracy? The Mumbai ATS, some people in the Army, the Cong-NCP government of Maharashtra, the UPA government in the centre, any or all of these?

He did not tell me who he thought was responsible and why, but instead raised the demand for a thorough enquiry at the highest level. He replied, 'After the trial, if the court acquits Purohit, there should be a thorough enquiry into the investigation, and it is about time we made the police and their masters accountable.'

Though he did not specify enquiry by whom, perhaps because the trial is still dragging on, I gathered he certainly didn't mean an enquiry at the level of the state government. It could either be a judicial enquiry or one initiated by an independent central agency.

Quite contrary to his usual frank and honest expression, I did not receive a very clear reply on my next two questions. I asked him whether he thought implicating Purohit was just an 'error of judgment' on the part of the investigators or part of a much larger political game plan.

His curt reply was, 'Can't say, let the trial be over.' This was slightly baffling as in the earlier question, he had particularly pointed at politics overwhelming investigations. I guess he did not wish to discuss 'specifics' while the trial was on.

Even on the question of sharing his impressions on the professionalism of ATS, he avoided a direct comment with the same plea, 'let the trial get over'.

Sensing that the lawyer was not so forthcoming in discussing the details of the case, and understandably so, I decided to steer the focus towards the larger issue on the table – that of Hindu terror, what it meant and what he thought of the entire narrative. While he had been curt and dismissive in sharing his thoughts on the trial, his reply on the question of Hindu terror was brief but quite telling.

I asked him how, as a legal luminary and a conscious citizen of India, did he look at the entire subject of Hindu terror. His answer was, 'Terror is a horrendous crime, and those responsible are despicable specimens barely fit to be called humans. I think phrases such as Hindu terror are obnoxious, but hardly surprising when you see the real reason why they were coined.'

These are the exact words of Salve. As I gathered, two points were conveyed very clearly from this. First, it was obnoxious to connect terror to a religion and coin a term prefixing the same. One doesn't need to explain that this conveyed a dangerous generalisation and was demeaning to the religion. Second, by indicating towards the 'real reason why', Salve 'did' agree that there were forces (political and maybe more) who had a predetermined design to portray Hindu religion in this sinister manner through the prefix.

His answer was sufficient indication that while abhorring terror in any form, Harish Salve did smell a political conspiracy, a well-thought-out 'intent' of pulling in the religion here. Indirectly, this also confirmed to my 'non-legal' mind that though he was cautious about discussing the merits of the case, he smelt a dirty game plan in Col Purohit's case.

In my conversation about the case and during the answers to several queries, I sensed a deep concern and perhaps even anger in Mr Salve on the issue of Hindu terror and the progress of the trial. Knowing that he has been representing the country in cases abroad, including the recent, very sensitive Kulbhushan Jadhav trial in the International Court of Justice, I wanted to understand his view on the international ramifications of Hindu terror, particularly during the time when it was 'the' headline every day. His answer reflected the same anger even though he did not mention Hindu terror specifically but spoke on the general narrative about India and Indians in the global platforms. He replied:

'There is an unfortunate tendency in the media to focus on India's so-called weaknesses. One example is calling India a dangerous country for women, when the global statistics show otherwise. Another is to portray

India as a bigoted country; nothing could be further from the truth. Communal politics has always been present – even from the days of the Constituent Assembly – and will continue to remain till politicians develop the moral standards which prevent them from exploiting the divides in society, whether it be caste, communalism or even poverty. But this should be put in perspective – on the contrary, some of us Indians proclaim in loud voices that we are a bigoted lot. That is most unfortunate.'

From his last comments, the sense I got from the entire conversation was this...

Though Harish Salve was being cautious and even economical with his words in discussing the actual case and hardly gave out anything on the merits of the case, he made it amply clear that the cases of Purohit and others, as also the very concept of Hindu terror, was overwhelmingly guided by politics, and that owing to this politics, the investigators (with particular reference to the Malegaon blast case) either lost focus or were 'made to lose' focus of the entire investigation. He did not stop at that but went a step further to demand a thorough investigation into the role of the 'investigators' and make them accountable for whatever may have gone wrong.

In short, Harish Salve stamped the conspiracy angle in the Malegaon case without saying it in so many words.

Since then, the trial has been progressing at a snail's pace, almost being in limbo for months. At times due to COVID related restrictions, and at other times due to various procedural reasons. The petition for quashing of UAPA continues to languish even as the trial in the regular case gathers dust in the special court. If and when the case progresses, I look forward to catching up with Mr Salve again to get further comments and his assessment of things again.

The whole idea of interacting with Harish Salve was to get a peek into the legal position of the case and get an idea of how strong the evidence stood its ground. From that standpoint, it turned out to be not just a fulfilling conversation but quite eye opening.

Why Purohit?

The Sinister Reports

All through the travels I undertook to understand the various unexplained twists and turns in the so-called Hindu terror plot, the helpful and not-so-helpful conversations I had with serving and retired officers, journalists and investigating officers, the one question that kept cropping from every quarter was, 'Why Purohit?' Why him? Many people had many explanations to offer, depending on their respective reading of the sequence of events, the background, the current politics and the many domestic and foreign forces that were at play. Some of them made intelligent guesses, some others were not privy to too many details but had been following the sequence of events from day one and thus tried to put two and two together. Yet others gave quick winks and spoke in unfinished sentences hinting that they knew much which could not be spoken.

So while the official details of the case, particularly from the prosecution's side, were already in the public domain, and I was able to piece together the experiences, the legal battle and the ups and downs of the case from Col Purohit's standpoint too, one question still kept lurking in the background. Why Purohit?

The best explanation came from those who neither knew the officers in the ATS nor had anything to do with Col Purohit. But they were clued in on the security scenario of the country and the activities of nefarious elements on a daily basis. Such people gave the most dispassionate dissection of the whole scenario. They were quick to discount some of the theories being forwarded by elements who were no doubt outraged by the politics over Hindu terror but were not quite privy to details. However, these sources had much to share with me. They brought me up to date with the background of India's precarious internal security dynamics which preceded the arrest of Purohit. This, coupled with the direction of politics at that point of time, started to make some sense. Piecing together the information from different sources, bit by bit, a lot seemed to 'fall in place'. My sources included serving and retired bureaucrats in

Delhi, investigating officers and a couple of analysts who had been following the course of events meticulously.

After all the meetings, discussions and correlations, what finally emerged was this:

Lt Col Prasad Shrikant Purohit had penetrated far too deep into the Jihadi networks which had started mushrooming all over India at that juncture. With help from sources cultivated over time, he had managed to have his men infiltrate the ranks so much so that information had started to trickle in almost real time.

With little to stop these networks from spreading their tentacles in the interiors of Kerala, Karnataka, Maharashtra, Bihar and Uttar Pradesh, it was becoming easier for them by the day to move men, arms and explosives from one corner of the country to the other in no time. The blasts, which occurred later in multiple cities in quick succession, are a grim indication of what was going on behind the scenes. These blasts in Gujarat, Uttar Pradesh, Maharashtra and the subsequent recovery of explosives have already been listed in the chapter, 'Its Hindu terror'.

To put it in a nutshell, the growing strength of SIMI, which was posing as a religious, social organisation of Muslim youth, was being tracked by Col Purohit and his team with a toothcomb. With meticulous planning and immense patience, Purohit and his associates had succeeded in piecing together the SIMI network right from north Kerala in the South up to Bihar and beyond. In fact, people in the know, claimed that Purohit had managed to crack sources across the border in Nepal.

Those running the show in Students' Islamic Network of India (SIMI) prided on the fact that it was a totally home-grown outfit consisting of young, educated Muslim boys who could argue and debate and interact in a manner befitting the generation. In other words, an Islamic body of youth for the modern times. But beneath this veneer of educated, modern Muslim youth, lay an organisation totally focused on the destruction of our nation, shattering communal peace and instilling a Jihadi mind-set in an entire generation of Muslim youth. SIMI was the banner of a deathly agent aimed at digging the grave of an upwardly mobile, aspirational generation of Indians by sowing the seeds of hatred and insecurity in their minds. It wore the posture of an innocuous student body, but for all practical purposes, SIMI was the India chapter of the Inter-Services Intelligence (ISI) of Pakistan; its motives, its plans, its manpower and 'operations' being funded and controlled from Rawalpindi.

It's not as if the goings-on in SIMI were totally off the radar. Intelligence officers and sleuths had been alerting their bosses in respective agencies regularly. The kind of meetings they held, their mad rush for recruitment of cadres from Kerala to Bihar to West Bengal was being flagged at regular intervals. However, these reports 'failed' to catch the eye of the bosses and their political masters for reasons best known to them.

It was at this crucial juncture that Col Purohit hit upon his most disturbing findings. Sources privy to his successive reports have confirmed that the army officer had hit upon leads which established the clear links of ISI with 'home-grown' SIMI cadres. Apparently there were clear evidences of their communication, their agents helping SIMI operatives to procure arms and ammunition, exchange of sensitive data, maps, locations and such other ground information. Subsequent blasts and recoveries did bring out to the whole world the extent of the flourishing network.

To the best of knowledge shared by my sources, Purohit and a couple of his associates were working on a minefield of information connecting the fast-growing links between the ISI, SIMI and the Maoist networks. Nepal was majorly on the radar. To say that the country was fast being sucked into a dragnet of extremist, violence-oriented operatives communicating through multiple-layered channels with the masterminds giving out directions and calling the shots from across the western border would not be an exaggeration. The state police forces were either ill-equipped to deal with this hydra-headed monster or bound by political lack of will for a crackdown. Or both.

Half a dozen officers, serving in the agencies and the

Ministry of Home Affairs, admitted to me that reports sent above about these nefarious networks and activities received very little attention, if at all.

The Turf War

While the political inertia or tendency to look the other way was definitely problematic, in the particular case of Lt Col Prasad Shrikant Purohit, a turf clash also seemed to have complicated things and exacerbated the situation. As a matter of practice, internal security comes under the domain of the Intelligence Bureau (IB). The standard practice is that any intelligence input which threatens to disturb law and order or jeopardise security must be flagged with the competent authority so it may be passed on to the law-enforcing agencies for necessary follow-up action. But enemies of the nation do not operate or execute their nefarious plans as per the turf division of the agencies. A crucial input can land on anybody's desk. In my conversations with half a dozen senior and middle-rank officers, belonging to both the Intelligence Bureau and the Military Intelligence, one thing became pretty clear. At least a couple of agencies were quite cut up about Col Purohit and his associates pursuing the hydra-headed Jihadi forces stepping up their activities all around. A former officer told me in a complaining tone that Purohit's tendency of not passing on the information to the IB and insisting on pursuing the leads himself was clearly not in keeping with standard practice. He said the moment he came upon something substantial, he should have reported it so that the information was shared with the IB which is the designated agency for internal security. None of the unfortunate consequences would have happened had he stuck to protocol and not insisted on overstepping the turf, argued the former IB officer.

But Purohit's associates, which included officers who had worked with him at various times and a couple of officers based in the home ministry, did not give much credence to the argument. A senior officer of the Military Intelligence and a former colleague of Purohit at once rejected the argument and said no intelligence man worth his salt would pass on any valuable lead until he had gotten to the bottom of the affair, and when it concerned the security of the country and its people, these water-tight turf divisions mattered little since the end purpose was the same – securing the nation.

'Let me explain to you, ma'am. Today, I am serving in an area where some mischievous activities have been reported, and I am informed by my sources. My first reaction would be to follow up the lead and report to my concerned in-charge. The same would then be passed on to the state agencies, the police etcetera. However, being an intelligence officer, I would not be so naïve as to pass just anything I learn from my sources or a piece of half-baked information at any cost. Not only that, if I have the smallest hint that there may be more valuable inputs coming or in the pipeline, I would be failing my duty if I didn't get to the bottom of the affair before stepping away,' he remarked.

While this officer's impassioned argument must be factored in as a field officer's point of view, the general opinion remained divided on the issue. A few serving and former officers did agree that Col Purohit may just have stepped on the toes of others, thus rubbing them the wrong way or neutralising some who could have been favourably disposed.

So much for overstepping the turf. The other common argument that came up during my entire interactions was of Purohit going or not going beyond his brief. As for the question: did he cross a line while pursuing his leads and was carried away to indulge in something legally not tenable? Like on the issue of the turf, opinion remained divided on this aspect as well. Most people I spoke to were of the view that if Col Purohit was working on a larger, well-thought-out plan, with full knowledge of his superiors (as claimed), then the legally tenable/ untenable barriers did not count for much. In the words of these functionaries, things were not always black or white in the complex world of military intelligence. Or any intelligence for that matter. There were always grey zones which would appear 'black' to an outsider who was not clued in on the full picture. It had to be evaluated in the larger scheme of things and any premature 'expose' of things would most certainly jeopardise the efforts.

This was the majority view. Though a senior, who was then in the command headquarters in Pune, differed with the view.

On all these questions, Purohit's legal team on their part maintained a consistent position that while these were interesting analyses for an academic debate, their client had been the victim of a conspiracy, and there was sufficient evidence to establish the same. All other questions of turf or legality were relevant to the world of intelligence but 'not' to the case in hand.

The NIA Act Vs The Communal Violence Bill

That the whole issue of Hindu terror impacted the politics of the country needs no reminder. In one way or the other, the issue was alive in our political discourse right from 2009 and gradually picked up pace in the UPA-II tenure. In the latter half of UPA-II, though the focus remained on corruption, prices, women's safety and the idea of a strong, resurgent India, the issue of Hindu terror entered the lexicon of electoral politics in a clear-cut manner without the 'ifs and buts' that were visible in the initial stages. But did the issue of Hindu terror also have influence on law making in Parliament? Yes, it did. But in a subtle, nuanced and certainly not-so-talked about manner.

Creating NIA

Following the Mumbai attack in 2008, the then Union Home Minister Shivraj Patil was unceremoniously removed on 30 November 2008. On the very same day, senior Congress Leader P Chidambaram took charge in North Block. It certainly wasn't the best of times to become the home minister of the country. The Mumbai attacks had shaken Indians not just in the country but all over the globe. It was like waking from a stupor. Faced with the enormity of the situation, P Chidambaram literally burnt the midnight oil to come up with two legislations aimed at curbing the rising threat of terror.

In less than a month of taking charge, to be precise on 17 December of the same year, the legislations had been moved on the floor of the House. These were the National Investigation Agency Bill and the Unlawful Activities (Prevention) Amendment Bill. The first legislation provided for the setting up of a new federal investigation agency for terror-related incidents. The central idea of setting up the agency was to by-pass the inordinate delays caused in investigating terror-related incidents which were almost always spread over more than one state, sometimes several states. By the time the state police and investigating teams of states established some kind of co-ordination with each other, the leads had already run cold. Also, there were too many obvious reasons why the teams of different states hardly ever came on the same page. Contrast this with the high-tech communication gadgets and technology being harnessed by terror modules and their bosses sitting across the border, it was as good as giving up the chase even before it started.

In the wake of the Mumbai attacks, all experts pointed to the need of a central agency which would not be tied down by territorial limitations of state police teams. It would operate across the country and would be empowered to follow up intelligence inputs on real-time basis and investigate all aspects including terror financing. It was the need of the hour, pointed out the experts. There was just one hurdle. And 'that' was a big one. None of the state governments were enthused about such an agency which could over-ride their powers of investigation by simply taking over a case related to internal security. Time was running out and states kept up the resistance. It didn't matter whether a state was ruled by the BJP, Congress, any of their allies or any other regional combine. States seemed to be on the same page. This was turf war. This was not about political ideologies. Even after the worst ever terror attack on Indian soil in Mumbai, states and their police were reluctant on the move and expressed it too. P Chidambaram may or may not have anticipated the resistance from the states, most particularly the regional parties within the UPA conglomerate. But it did threaten the fate of the proposed

Bill which the Home Minister was keen to pass in the winter session itself.

Of course, for those who believe in googling and going by the stated positions, the BJP played the perfect opposition by voting in favour of the NIA Bill while criticising it on the floor of the house and even outside. During the debate on the floor of the two houses, senior BJP members called it 'too little, too late' or even a 'half-baked job'. But what happened behind the curtain was much more significant. If not for some senior leaders of BJP in Parliament, the Bill proposing to establish the National Investigation Agency would have never seen the light of day. There were moments when it appeared that the Bill was destined to fall with the left on the one hand and the regional powers on the other having their own respective set of objections.

At this point, it was a section of the BJP leadership which rose to the occasion and signalled the home minister to go ahead with the legislation. At the back of the move was the BJP's conviction that a federal investigation agency was not only essential but overdue; the kind of multi-layered, hydra-headed terror threat the country was facing could not be left to the state police forces or their anti-terror wings. First, they weren't trained or equipped for it. Second, even if one or two states were picking up, it was nothing less than a nightmare to conduct probes against these highly motivated, high-tech enabled modules when they fanned out into different states and cities. While these arguments were heard in the public domain in the run-up to the placing of the Bill, what was not spoken in so many words was the fact that quite often state governments did not support the agencies to go full force against the suspects but instead let investigations go slack.

So, with all these considerations in the background, the Bill enabling the creation of a National Investigation Agency (NIA) was passed in the Lok Sabha and then soon after in Rajya Sabha, just three weeks after the Mumbai attacks which scarred the nation like no other terror incident.

Of course, the NIA Bill was not the only legislation to be placed. It was coupled with the amendments to the Unlawful Activities Prevention Act (UAPA) which provided stringent measures to fight terror. The provisions were strongly opposed by the left parties on grounds of civil/human rights. Here too the BJP came to stand with the government and helped pass the Bill. But not before rubbing it in that the UPA had allegedly diluted the war on terror by repealing the Prevention of Terrorism Act (POTA).

UPA's Communal Violence Bill

A couple of years after the NIA Bill, the UPA government proposed another legislation which was set to become a bone of contention for a pretty long time. This one was a brainchild of the National Advisory Council (NAC) which was mandated to discuss policies and programmes of the UPA government.

According to a report in *India Today* online, 'the proposed Communal Violence Bill, which was discussed at the National Integration Council (NIC) meet... intends to prevent and control targeted violence against the Scheduled Castes, the Scheduled Tribes and religious and linguistic minorities....According to the draft bill prepared by the National Advisory Council (NAC), the legislation is intended to enhance state accountability and correct discriminatory exercise of state powers in the context of identity-based violence.'

The Prevention of Communal and Targeted Violence (Access to Justice and Reparations) Bill, 2011 aimed at defining communal and targeted violence, sanction for public servants for 'dereliction of duty' and provided for the setting up of a National Authority for Communal Harmony, Justice and Reparation (NACHJR). The Bill prompted long debates in the media; much was written in the newspapers and the digital online media. Activists and civil society members, who were instrumental in drafting the legislation, held many seminars and discussions too. However, this time, the Bill failed to cut ice with BJP, the principal opposition party, though there were many others who were equally suspicious.

Even before it came for discussion in the National

Integration Council meet referred to in the earlier para, no less than fifty-odd amendments had already been made in the original draft since it was first put up on the website. The most common concern was with the terminology 'internal disturbance'. By the definition in our constitution, if any incident/s of violence was termed 'internal disturbance' it would come under the ambit of Article 355. This was something no state government would ever agree to. Sensing the damage, the clause was deleted from the draft.

But there was a bigger bone of contention – that related to the presumption about the 'victims' of communal or targeted violence. The Bill clearly presumed that the 'people' who were victims of communal or targeted violence were religious and/or linguistic minorities. This, in turn, obviously envisaged that in every such case of violence, the perpetrator would always be considered to be from the majority community no matter what the facts on the ground. The BJP, which was opposed to the Bill from its very inception, termed it a Congress ploy to woo minorities. In an article, the party's frontline leader Arun Jaitley wrote, 'This draft bill proceeds on the presumption that communal trouble is created only by members of the majority community and never by a member of the minority community.'

There was much back and forth on the issue, sometimes in the public domain but more often in the background. There were also some reports in the media that the very idea of the Bill was inspired by the Gujarat riots of 2002 and hence the thrust on the 'minorities'. It may be relevant to mention here that the first draft of the Bill was prepared by the NAC in 2005 itself and also placed on the floor of Rajya Sabha, though, of course, it could not be passed and hence remained there in limbo. Importantly, a legislation placed on the floor of Rajya Sabha does not lapse with the end of a session. It stays alive and can be revived if and when required.

While the first Bill of 2005 (during UPA-I) was rejected on account of various contentious provisions, the second attempt in 2011 definitely looked like a more serious move. The clear message from the BJP, articulated most clearly by Arun Jaitley as mentioned above, ensured that the Bill would not see the light of day even six years after the first move. Though the last nail in the coffin of the vexed legislation was yet to be driven. Before I come to that, just to give a brief timeline of the uncleared legislation, the Bill was introduced for the first time in Rajya Sabha on 5 December 2005. It was referred to the Standing Committee on 1 January 2006. Exactly a year later, the Standing Committee submitted its report on 13 December 2006. As pointed out, there was much back and forth before the government finally gave in and withdrew the Bill on 5 February 2014, in the last Parliament session of the UPA regime.

Perhaps no other Bill, except the vexed Women's Reservation Bill, had such a chequered record. Sample this: After the Standing Committee submitted its report in December 2006, there were multiple notices given in the House such as in March 2007, December 2008, February 2009, December 2009 and again in February 2010.

After so many failed attempts, the NAC took a step back and re-drafted the provisions. A report in the *Times of India* on 15 July 2010 titled 'NAC to redraft communal violence bill' read: 'The National Advisory Council on Wednesday decided to completely recast the communal violence bill, which had got mired in a protracted debate between civil society and the bureaucracy.'

That 'recast' as reported by the paper did not pacify the opposition, though it did go a step further in addressing the objection of 'disturbed area' which had triggered an acrimonious debate on the federal structure.

We know very well that the recast or rework did not help the government in getting the Bill through. While the top BJP leadership stuck to its arguments, the final nail in the Bill's coffin was driven by the then Chief Minister of Gujarat, Narendra Modi, who sealed the fate of the legislation for good. Knowing that the UPA government was ready to push for the bill in its last winter session (December 2013), Modi wrote a terse letter to Prime Minister Manmohan Singh on the morning of the first day of the session. He termed the Communal Violence Bill 'ill-conceived, poorly drafted and a recipe for disaster'. Modi's objections pertained to 'attempt to encroach upon the domain of states' and that 'religious and linguistic identities would become more reinforced'. He also raised 'operational issues' and remarked that it would 'adversely impact the morale of public servants and law-enforcing agencies'. After that strong-worded frontal attack, the Bill lay in limbo and was finally withdrawn in February.

Now to come back to our subject, the obvious question that arises here is what did this entire trajectory or timeline of the stalled Communal Violence Bill have to do with Col Purohit's case or even the subject of Hindu terror? Well, it did. And this is something which failed to strike most political observers and even those hovering closely around the powers-that-be. Of course, some did get an inkling and co-related both the seemingly unrelated legislations, but that was largely in hindsight and limited to a miniscule section of political watchers or a small handful. So how did the two legislations relate or impact each other?

As indicated above, the Bill enabling the setting up of the National Investigation Agency could not have come by had the top line of the BJP's parliamentary team not come forward to shield the government from the opposition emanating from the UPA's own allies and other regional parties. But that gesture of co-operation, inspired by the conviction that only a federal agency like the NIA could avert another Mumbai attack in future, could not be expected in case of the Communal Violence Bill. And the objection was not limited to the alleged tilt towards minorities. In fact, the UPA was ready to make amendments and concessions in the contentious sections had the opposition indicated willingness to discuss.

By the time the NIA Bill was passed in Parliament, Col Purohit and the others had already been in jail for over two months. But until then, no one, including the BJP leadership, could fathom the wider political ramifications of the Hindu terror theory. Nor did they imagine that the frontline leadership of the RSS would be put under cloud for the same. The damage potential of the issue for the entire *Sangh Parivar*[15] (Sangh family) and its supporters had not been gauged until then by the BJP leaders. Nor did they foresee the possibility that Hindu or Saffron terror would become not just a daily headline but take centre stage in the political discourse or narrative to target the Sangh Parivar.

But as time progressed, the entire gamut of challenges started unfolding before the BJP leadership. Top RSS leaders' names were floated back to back and clouded in the

---

15 *Sangh Parivar:* the collection of Hindu nationalist organisations led by the Rashtriya Swayamsevak Sangh (RSS)

light of terror. The BJP was continuously being saddled by its own ideological family and the challenges just seemed to keep mounting. Meanwhile, UPA had returned to power with the Congress bagging a much larger share of seats. That gave the UPA renewed confidence to push for the Communal Violence Bill hanging fire in Rajya Sabha. As the government listed the Bill in every other session, the BJP and the RSS top brass went over and over the developments of the preceding years, especially since 2008. And they arrived at only one conclusion. That, in the light of the dreadful Mumbai attacks, their leadership did everything to help the Congress get the NIA Bill passed in Parliament. However, instead of going after the 'real' terrorists who had spread their tentacles to the far corners of India, the NIA instead went after the RSS leadership and what the Sangh Parivar termed as the staunch nationalists. The entire Sangh Parivar and even those who weren't part of the Parivar but felt inclined to its ideology saw in this a game plan of the Congress party to discredit, defame and destabilise its biggest political challengers. One may go into the NIA folders on a case-to-case basis and contest the argument on the basis of investigation, intelligence, etcetera but that's how politics works. It's a battle of perceptions, and the perception had already been strengthened. So, in a classic case of once bitten twice shy, the BJP hardened its stance with every parliament session and 'ensured' that the Communal

Violence Bill would never see the light of day. The party and more so its ideological parivar was certain that, like the NIA, this would become another tool of the ruling dispensation to go after them big time.

Hindu Terror Politics and the Watershed 2014 Polls

The 2014 Lok Sabha polls threw up many firsts such as the first BJP Prime Minister to win a clear majority, also the first Prime Minister to win a clear mandate in over three decades and also the first Chief Minister in many years to take oath as Prime Minister. To this day, it remains one of the most discussed, analysed and written-about general election ever in the national as well as global media vis-à-vis our country. Everybody has their take on what led to such a decisive mandate for Narendra Modi. Corruption, political drift and policy paralysis are the most commonly quoted factors. Rightly so. But when we scratch below the surface, it becomes clear that issues like Hindu terror also contributed in a major way to build up that (first) disappointment and (later) anger against the UPA regime. It created an impression that the centre was going after people who did not suit the Congress' scheme of things and that these people were invariably from the majority community. Perception also gained ground that Hindus were being slighted and targeted at every stage. That this was not just drawing room political gossip or conjecture became clear to me during my extensive travels in the build-up to the 2014 general elections. In fact, it was the Congress party itself which put a stamp on the observations of field reporters like me when its report on the drubbing in the polls spelt this out in so many words. The much talked about report, often referred to as Antony report (as the committee was headed by senior congressman AK Antony), laid a lot of stress on the fact that the voters had started looking at the Congress party as pandering only to the minority community at the cost of the interest of the majority thus pushing the party to its worst ever Lok Sabha tally, far below even the 1977 post-Emergency election. The 1977 election was often referred to as a wash-out for the Congress, but it still won 154 seats (mostly down south), whereas in 2014, the party scored just 44, a clear 110 down.

Needless to say, majority and minority in common political parlance are euphemisms for Hindu and Muslim respectively. Regardless, whether it was intended or inadvertent, the UPA government led by the Congress party was looked upon as anti-Hindu by a chunk of the electorate. And in creating this perception, one of the many potent factors was the discourse over the Hindu terror. So yes, the issue did have substantial political ramifications.

The political dispensation changed in 2014 with Narendra Modi taking charge but the issue of false equivalences certainly did not. The biggest concern for a large section of nationalist Indians was that the bogey of Hindu terror became a shield for Jihadi terror which was raising its ugly head menacingly in far corners of the country. That section remains worried as a segment of the intelligentsia (mostly identified by its left-oriented leanings) continue to raise the bogey of Hindu Taliban and Hindutva terrorists even to this day while the nationalist segment claims that the fight against the false equivalences continues.

PHOTO GALLERY

Col Purohit in Police Custody.

Picture Courtesy: India.com

Col Purohit during his trial.

Picture Courtesy: Navbharat Times

Col Purohit dons uniform for the first time after being granted bail by SC.
Picture Courtesy: ANI

Col Purohit with his wife, Aparna Purohit.
Picture Courtesy: The Bridge Chronicle